This book is dedicated to:
My children Elizabeth and Ian, without whom, there is no life; and
My husband Dave, who has found the courage to look inside
himself before it was too late.
I love you all so much.

Forward

This book was started 59.5 years ago (as of today). I should have called it the "Book of Kathi", but that just seems so lofty and over the top. The truth of it all is that, not unlike other authors, I have been writing in my brain 24/7/365 for as long as I can remember. It really is getting the words to page that is most difficult. Especially difficult when making your first attempt at writing. There were days when I felt like I could write for hours. There were days/weeks/months where nothing would come to me at all. Every time I would re-read something, I would change it. Spinning wheels, spinning round.

Heart Bleed means just that. My heart bleeding onto paper. At first I thought "who cares what you think about this or that?" You may not. But, I had work to do with my writing. There were stories that I wanted to tell, people I wanted you to know, lives that had meaning that would go unremarked, but who changed the life of at least one person – me. I've always believed that those who love the most, give the most. I wanted to celebrate the efforts of some of those I've known to do that. You may not know that person, but I bet you know one like them. And, you may be that person to someone else. You deserve the recognition.

I also wanted to tell some stories that speak to and for those who feel they have no voice. There are so many of us out there. So many people who endure personal tragedies and hardships who are never celebrated. Some are hidden away, some hide themselves away, but most go about their day to day activities with part of their souls sealed off in protection. If reading my stories helps or reassures just one person, then all of this will have been worthwhile.

Please don't think I believe I am all that and a bag of chips. I've already been told that my blog, on which this book is based, reads like a Lifetime Movie, or that it jumps all over the place – very much a stream of consciousness effort. And that maybe so. But it's real. And as honest as I can make it.

None of us want to pass through life without leaving something of themselves behind. I have two children, but as proud of them as I am, they have their own lives to build, their own marks to leave in the sand. This is mine. Chaotic. Disorganized. Real. Some things may be hard to read, some things may be so incredibly boring that you wonder why you are making the effort. But I do believe that we all learn from each other. Perhaps there is something in this book that will make things clearer, or better, or happier for you. I hope so. But if not, I've done what I set out to do for myself. Create something tangible. For myself.

I've been blessed with a wonderful supporting cast over the years. I can't thank them enough. Some you will meet in this book, others you will meet (if the books gods decree it possible) in future books. But not a person who has been a part of my life passed through without leaving their imprint. So, thank you to all who have been a part of my life. Were it not for the experiences we had together, my life would have been … well, maybe less interesting. But it would not have been the same. Nothing is coincidental.

I do need to forewarn you that I am not your normal author. There is some NSFW writing in here (nothing erotic or anything – that scares me) but rather some language that you may find offensive. Just a heads up. I consider it all perfectly normal, as anyone who knows me will attest.

Also, I speak of real people whom I have asked permission of to be part of the stories. Without exception I have been given that permission by them. I have not used last names for the most part because they are simply irrelevant to the purpose.

And with that, I leave you with Heart Bleed. Each chapter is an "essay" of sorts, a commentary on something. When I went to edit, I thought I would rearrange things a bit as early chapters are very short, and chapters lengthen as I dive into certain subjects. It was a process (thank you Jason Garrett for instilling that insidious thought), and a development. There is no conventional storyline, so reading the ending first (as I do with my ADD) will mean nothing.

Peace!

Kathi Haacke Morehead
May 2014

The Why Of It All

2014. Thank God. I made it. If ever there was a year I want in the rear view mirror, it's 2013. Yes, I know the old wives tale that I will bring myself bad luck by saying this, but I don't hold a lot of stock in that. Masturbating has never made any of my friends blind, though a LOT of them wear dark sunglasses. So .. meh on old wives' tales.

I can't even say I had a bad year in 2013. There were some more than stellar moments in it. Like .... seeing myself in a television show. Netflix's "House of Cards" to be exact. Or, applauding my son (who didn't have a very inspiring high school career) when he scored all A's and made Deans List at UMBC. Or, proudly watching my daughter take a stand for something she believed in, even at the risk of professional stagnation. Yep! 2013 was aces in those departments.

2013 became not so great on April 20 when I went blind in my right eye. See, I learned a valuable lesson. Do not throw out to the universe anything that you're not willing to bear coming back to you. One of my favorite Kathi-isms was "I'd rather stick pins in my eyes than …." I used this expression a lot to express disgust with someone or something, and is one of those lame ass comments I used to make in stupid conversation. You won't hear me saying I'd rather have pins stuck in my eyes ever again because .. well ... when that DOES happen, it sucks real time. I guess it really is a case of be careful what you wish for. Or say. All I know is I've learned my lesson, and I'm not wishing for anything. Okay, that is patently absurd, don't believe it for a moment. I don't.

Anyway, yes, I was graced with a 90% retinal detachment in my right eye and God, Dr. Ha (yes) and the rest of the staff at

Hopkins Wilmer Eye Institute were able to put Humpty Dumpty back together again. Really glad to see that gone, and going blind is now OFF my bucket list.

Death. It was a pretty awful year with respect to that, but at 59, I'm really not sure that situation will improve much. Close friends losing young children, parents, siblings. Losing people you love. Does it ever seem right? And do those we lose deserve it? No, I think not. Ah life. You unpredictable son of a bitch. If I believed in payback, I'd be down on my knees apologizing for whatever karmic sin I'd committed, demanding you return life. But I don't. I believe we chart our own paths long before we start to walk them. So, on some level, I've come to terms with mortality. I really don't want it tested further. At least not with the same intensity it showed in 2013. I got the lessons you sought to teach me 2013. Let me prove it in 2014.

And, as an aside, death is also off my bucket list. Just sayin.

So this, right here, right now, is how I begin. I'm going to write. What a crazy ride this will be. What this will develop into – at this moment in time, I have no idea. But I can guarantee some tears, some laughs, some "OMG did she really SAY that" moments, honesty, and probably a few really stupid observations. But .. it's genuine. And these days, not sure we can say that about a lot of things.

Get ready to fly your freak flag freely. Welcome aboard the crazy train!

Did I Just Guilt Myself?

I'm sitting here in my bedroom, on my bed, with all four cats. I am home from work, have changed into my bathrobe, and have no clue what to do next. Do I throw on my work out clothes and head to the gym, or do I take the day off (Wednesday and Sunday according to Jillian, who I consulted for my fitness plan)? I could fall back on my "day off" excuse even though it's not Wednesday or Sunday, but my wanting to rest these old bones absolutely violates my need to whip myself for not wanting to do it. Because, after all, isn't being smart, sexy, sassy, and healthy the way I am supposed to be living?

Hey me. I've got news for you - it hurts to move around sometimes. You need to accept that. You can probably get some of it fixed, but what about this whole aging gracefully thing you've sworn to do?

Conscience be gone! I think overall I'm not doing badly (though I'm far from being able to run a half marathon, or ignore free fries on someone's plate). My health is way good for someone who is overweight, smoked more than I should have, and is on the downside of 50. Seriously. I'm in good shape physically - despite myself.

But not everything moves the way I'd like it to. Not as easily. No one would ever use the word graceful to describe me (or athletic or coordinated .. you get the picture) but I'm kicking it okay for 59. The problem is that I have the self-discipline of a gnat. Get the picture?

Working out today requires changing into clothes, leaving the house, driving in a cold car the less than a mile it takes to get to the gym, going into the gym and hoping that one of the three treadmills they have is available (yeah, small town) and then going for it. When I'm finished, I'm going to walk outside in the January evening sans coat, hat, or anything else that can't be shed because my body is heated to a core temperature of a million degrees. I'll start my car, put all the windows down, and drive the mile back home.

By then, I'll be freezing and will take a shower and go to bed. Oh, let's not forget the Advil I'll take for the aches and pains. So, I will have endured ALL of this so that I don't feel guilty.

Ummm. Let's see. All of that ….. nice warm bed watching TV ….. all of that ….. nice warm bed watching TV. Really, this is a no brainer, don't you think?

If you figure it out, let me know. I'll be back after I run.

Definition Issues

It's January here in Maryland. Now. If I wanted a snowy, below freezing January, I'd move to Maine or Minnesota or any of the other cold states that start with the letter M. But I don't. I live here because it's temperate. We used to get four changes of season. Not so much now.

But I've come across an interesting observation. Our winter is being described as "fucking cold". Excuse me while I get literate here, but isn't that an oxymoron?

What exactly does "fucking cold" mean? I'm serious here. The words fucking and cold seem to be descriptively at cross purposes. And not to sound unladylike or anything, but when I think about bumping uglies, cold is not an attribute I'd embrace. So, what does "fucking cold" mean? Is it a geographical thing? Like in Maine it means too cold to go ice fishing? Or in Arizona, 80 degrees? I dunno.

But I can tell you that right now, here in my house, the "fucking cold" standard is the point at which alcohol driven warm drinks have no impact on my psyche other than the mating of two cheeks and an ice cube masquerading as a toilet seat. THAT is fucking cold.

Frozen Tears

Yeah, it's snowing again, and since this wasn't on the radar when I left on Friday, I'm without my work laptop. So, it leaves me with time on my hands. I could clean the oven or do laundry, but I'd much rather sit here and feel ridiculously sorry for myself.

On this day in 1961, my ex-husband was born. The litany of egregious experiences that would greet this happy, sentimental child would be almost unbelievable. A much loved older sister, and only sibling, would hang herself when he was 11 because her parents refused to accept that she was gay. To compensate for that loss and with the belief that God had deserted them, his parents would bring unspeakable horror to his young life by embracing the world of free sex and swinging - to the extent of having someone take both his virginity and part of his soul at 13. This, of course, his parents' effort to insure his heterosexuality. His parents celebrated their oneness with their golden boy by including him in their swinging parties during his teens. His father would hang an explicit naked picture of his mother in the foyer of their home. High school was an agony for him.

With seeming complete disregard for him, his parents climbed into bottles and never looked back. Never helped this golden boy, believing he had been given all keys necessary for a successful life. Never knew, understood, or cared that their son's emotional life was stunted at age 11. But, his will was great when he was young, and he built a persona that drew everyone he met into his circle. Witty, musical, whimsical, sentimental - always a believer in the knight on the white horse.

This was the man I met, fell in love with, laughed and loved with, and who gave me my most precious daughter. This is the man who I watched crawl into a bottle himself, reject

13

adulthood, and turn his bi-polar anger on me and our daughter. This was the man I had to leave to save myself and my baby. A man who would cut us out of his life without love or support for 13 years, only to resurface, beg for us to return to him (after three more unsuccessful marriages), begin rebuilding a relationship with his daughter. The man who, after the suicide of his father, would run from a Maryland DUI to Vegas, marry again, decorate his Christmas tree, go into his bedroom, put a gun to his head and end it for all of us.

The last email I received from him was 8 months prior to his death. All it said was "marry me". I didn't even respond. This shames me on some primal level.

In spite of it all, I bless this day because he was born. The gifts he gave me of love and laughter will always be in my heart. The greatest gift of all, our daughter .. I can't imagine the battles he fought, and I've finally given up trying to sort it all out. Sometimes the most important thing is just remembering love. We all have plenty of pain to live with. Blame. Angst. I punished myself for his life and death for a very long time until I realized I'd given him the best I had to give. It was his contract, not mine. So I am fortunate that only love and some sadness remains where anger could easily have been.

Rest in well deserved peace. Heal. We will forgive, but never forget.

Winter Desolation

Ugh.

Christmas decorations that are still up in February.

Is there anything more bereft than Christmas decorations in February? They just look so sad, like puppies at the pound.

I wonder why they're still up? Are the owners too lazy? Or depressed that the holidays are over? I get that. After Christmas, there's a long dark deep freeze upon us. I can understand not wanting to face that. I hate it.

But seeing depleted wreaths of pine deteriorating, with ribbons blowing aimlessly; or streams of multi-colored lights, always missing at least one lit bulb just seems so excruciatingly lonely and forgotten.

Much like awful plastic flowers in cemeteries.

Perhaps it's a metaphor bigger than I can comprehend.

Drool

So, today a young friend of mine commented on how, enjoying her 30's, she was happy to see that more women were embracing natural health, fitness, and aging. I had to think about this for a little bit. At double that age, I immediately bristled. A natural conditioning, yes? Good god, at 18, I didn't think I'd see 30 ("never trust anyone over 30" says the White Rabbit) so the idea of doubling that, and being here to see it, is almost incredible to me. Let alone "naturally". I puzzled over that a bit. For the sake of this conversation, we'll assume that means "no cosmetic intervention".

And then I felt a sense of pride that I've not felt since bra burning. Way to go Baby Boomers! No. We haven't solved the political, economic, and world hunger issues we thought we would, but by god .. we have learned to age! We are setting the new standard! In the past, it was all about preserving our youth, kinda like putting your virginity in mothballs for a re-do. I admit - a year ago I was all about getting my eyes lifted. I'm not even sure why. I can think of other ways to spend $6k, like renting a really REALLY nice getaway shack on some island whose name you can't pronounce that requires a dolphin sled to get there.

I work with folks whose average age is somewhere in the 30s. I am not the oldest one there, but damn close. Thing is, I never FEEL that old. Okay, maybe when hubby is giving me a hard time or one of my kids is going through something difficult. But on the whole, I have felt very Jason Mraz for the past six years. Hanging with these wonderful people has made me realize that we are truly as old as we feel. And it's given me a reason to take care of myself.

The generation before me didn't expect to live much past 75 or so. I think my parents were actually surprised when they did. My generation doesn't expect to live much past 85. So I guess some of us will make it past there, God willing. Unfortunately, with the advent of technology, we are dealing with issues of law and mortality that I think will make an already cluttered gray area even more difficult to negotiate. But, I do believe that we are accepting that 60 is the new 40 (or is that just my own need to validate?), and learning to take better care of ourselves. That includes not looking for the latest and greatest plastic surgeon who will make you look like Bruce Jenner or Joan Rivers - faces stretched so tightly you expect them to crack. And it means taking better care of ourselves.

I love the Robin Wright and Jamie Lee Curtis's of the world. I love that they are free, as women, to be who they are and want to be, not who they think they need to be. I know that I'm giving it my best shot. Always, always ... life comes down to the "be true to yourself" adage. We run, but we cannot hide.

So some advice to the 30 somethings .. live each day and respect yourselves. And let me know how you're doing when you get to 60 something. You'll recognize me. I'll be the one strapped in a seat, drooling on myself .. but chances are I'll be braless in a tie dye T shirt. Right on!

The Shoulds

This is called "No, you really don't have to". Just so you know.

I read something quite near to my heart this evening. An essay on the word "should" as part of your internal dialogue.

I *should* go to church this weekend.
I *should* go to the gym.
I *should* call/write/visit so and so.

No. You really don't have to. "Should" ... according to who? Coming from anyone, including your gut, "should" is, at best, a suggestion, at worst - an accusation. You don't need that crap, I don't need that crap. It's a sentence for a presumed offense, and you are your own judge, jury, and sentence enforcer.

Should suggests that you we need to do something self-imposed, almost as a punishment. And what happens next? Guilt. Then you might try bargaining with yourself to present a defense, but it never helps. You still feel guilty for a "should" unfulfilled, and you stand a more than average chance of being pissed off with yourself for making yourself feel guilty. It's the proverbial hamster wheel.

I *should* go to the gym. But I'm tired from working all day, and I'm not gonna go. Intuitive solution? Bring on the cheesy bread and milkshake. I need to fuel up so that I am at full strength to beat myself up. Ahh the joys of an insidious and completely useless cycle of self-abuse.

So, I am banning *should* from my life. If I want to do something, I'll do it. If I don't want to do it ... screw it. I'm not wasting my precious energy beating myself up over expectations that may or may not be healthy. My moral compass is set. I know right from wrong. And isn't that the final answer? Not some

19

dumb guilt induced expectation. Rock on. From here on out, I do because I WANT and it makes me happy. Give it some thought. It's okay to do just for you.

ADDENDUM: So you know. I took my advice. It took me several months to convince myself of the worthiness of this advice, but once I got it, I got it. Give it some thought.

Chicken Caesar Salad

OCD ALERT! (Just, by the way, one of the many mental illnesses I will try to ascribe to myself. I feel like a walking, functioning, mental hypochondriac.)

It snowed again. So, mid-afternoon I went out and shoveled the walk, steps, and around hubby's car so he can get out in the morning (in unison now: what a good wife!). The snow was soft, very fluffy snow - very easy to move. And I put down snow melt/salt. My walks and parking spaces looked better than any on the block. I was so proud of myself. Now it's snowing again.

You can't even tell that I did all that work, and I wouldn't even care but my OCD is off the charts again. Do I go out and shovel it now, wait a couple of hours, what to do, what to do? I don't want it to get heavier, so I may just wait till it stops and go out and shovel again. My anxiety is so bad, you'd think we were talking about being sworn in as the POTUS or taking my clothes off with the light on or something.

You know, I'm not adverse to working from home, but I HATE being snowbound - and we are, and it will likely last through at least tomorrow afternoon. It's that feeling of knowing I can't do something, rather than not wanting to do something. All of a sudden, I'm feeling like I can't live without a trip to Walmart. WTF is that. No one wants to go to Walmart - unless you're trolling for pics of the most challenged fashionistas EVAH. It's the knowing I cannot do that right now without risking life and limb - if at all. I hate limits. I absolutely hate them. And being snow bound, through no fault of my own, is a very VERY big limit.

A guy got arrested for using a flame thrower in the Midwest because he was so tired of shoveling snow. He thought melting it would work. I think it's genuis. And I'm trying to understand why it's illegal. And this is only day 1. Good god, by day 2 will I be renting a dogsled and hooking hubby to it? Mush! Mush! [To be clear, this is not a fetish issue, but rather a transportation one.]

More than anything I want a chicken caesar salad from the local place that delivers. I feel as though I cannot live without it.

Sucks to be me today.

Reinvention?

Is it possible to "find yourself" at 59, or is it simply a reinvention?

Today I had a conversation with my son. He said "Mom, can you believe I'm only three semesters away from graduation?" Thinking practically I responded with a litany of life stages he would be facing after graduation - career, family, mortgage, saving for education, yada, yada, yada. I think back to the times we despaired during his high school years, wondering how this all would turn out. To say that he has risen above and succeeded beyond our expectations is an understatement. I am delighted that he takes pride in his accomplishments. He is so far ahead in the game of Life than I was at his age. Yet, instead of tamping down the reality he will face and encouraging his excitement at the future, I heaped more on his plate. Ugh. Sometimes I think I've become the more unpleasant part of my parents - the tired, worried, cautionary, killjoy. I will make that up to my son, but to do so, I first need to make it up to me so I "get" it.

Not unlike everyone, I've been a chameleon most of my life. In college, I wanted to win a Pulitzer for news reporting - but I had to pay bills, so I became a secretary. When I was a legal secretary, I wanted to be a paralegal. When I was a paralegal, I wanted to be an attorney. We adapt to our circumstances because real life dictates. Dreams are pooh poohed as irresponsible, do your job. Don't follow your heart, it's not practical.

Well, finally, I've decided to follow my heart. I spend quality time with myself. I set up a comfy nook, and started writing. Really writing. I have no idea where I will go with it, but my heart is lighter because I've taken that first step toward following my heart. I'm not sure I can call it "ego", though I can't lie and say there is not a piece of me that wants to be appreciated as an author; but, it really is bringing me to a safe and happy spot by doing this. So, I am debating whether this is about finding myself or simply reinventing. I don't know yet, but I will figure it out. In the meantime, I will go back to my son and ask him what he wants to do after graduation so that he doesn't waste time not following his dream

Believe me. I will do everything I can to make sure that happens.

Scraping the Bottom of the Bell Jar

I suffer from chronic depression. Of course I've known it all my life, just never had a name for it until I was 'diagnosed'. Everyone gets depressed. I know this. I've read a plethora of information on it. But today was one of those Plath kind of days. I'm pretty sure only someone who has read and understood Plath and/or been severely depressed can really understand it. I don't think there are words descriptive enough to be honest. It's the kind of day where you keep falling off the cliff again and again and again, no matter what you do, or who you talk to, or what pain killing extent you go to. Sometimes the drop comes at you quickly, other times the wait seems interminable. It's basically the same amount of time it takes to produce a tear – but even that is a hopeless release.

I'm not suicidal like Sylvia Plath, and never intend to be. My ego wouldn't let me. Which is the greater hell? There is something inside, I think I might call it my soul, that keeps my feet moving even when my heart freezes and refuses warmth. The hardest thing to live with, for me, is a perception of hypocrisy in things that I do. Perhaps that speaks to the conflict within, I'm not sure.

What I am sure of is that I love life, I am loved greatly by those by matter, and that I will see another day. I pray that it is not as dark as today, but there are no guarantees, and perhaps it will be another slugfest for me. But in the end, I know that even as I scrape the bottom of the jar, there is still more than enough left to make it all worthwhile.

Peace.

Dating Sites

So, I'm watching TV, and I have found my new nominees for stupid: dating site commercials.

"God can use any tool ..." ... What? I'm not kidding you. That's from a Christian Mingle dating service ad. So many ways to take that if you want.

"She's a cougar!"
"Never in my life did I think I'd find a *younger man.*" ... Our Time dating service ad. Over 50 years old only please.

"But I told her eHarmony had all the hot babes!"
"Now Caroline, I never said that." [Gratuitous lecherous grandfather to granddaughter who resembles Heidi with a lisp] ... eHarmony.com

Cows chewing grass while human male or female walks forlornly through rows of corn: "Do you think [he/she] will ever find love?"
"Not as long as [he/she] keeps hanging out with us all the time!" .... Farmers only.com

I have nothing against online dating sites. Let's preface this whole conversation with that.

I do have an aversion to insulting, ignorant comments. Not everyone who is single is unhappy. Some are single by choice. Some very much want to find meaningful relationships. You have to wonder who brilliantly conjured up the dating site niche.

As a woman over 50, the "cougar" commercial makes me

want to punch that woman in the face. First she says she has to "call it like it is" and shares what a great body he has. Totally subjective call there, by the way sweet cheeks. I totally questioned her credibility right there. Then he calls her a cougar. I totally question his intentions right there. All the while throwing out buzz phrases like the ease of understanding the nuances of their lives [translation: anyone under 50 just cannot possibly understand what it's like to be single, divorced, or never married]. What happens here? You're single, female, over 50, and all of a sudden you become a complete idiot, willing to share how desperate you are??? [Editor note: as of the date of print, this commercial has been pulled. Thank god.]

Farmers only.com … I was raised in an agricultural area. In all of my life, never have I seen anyone walking *alone* in a cornfield who wasn't working, if you catch my drift. Obviously the cows are smarter. They are always together. Same with fish. They swim in schools. I wonder if there is a fisherman only.com that I'm unaware of … it's probably in beta stage.

What can you say about Pop Pop pimping out Heidi. Disturbing that a 10 year old is discussing such matters with her teacher. And that she came up with the "hot babes" thing? Seriously?

Christian Mingle … I have serious questions about the legitimacy of organized religion. Now we have people claiming God guided them through all those winks and emails to just the right person. It makes me wonder if "Would you live in a bus and home school scads of my children without taking birth control or your bi-polar medication if God told you to" is on the questionnaire.

And of course, there's Ashley Madison. "The" dating site for married folks. At least they are honest. They're bored and want to play, and not particularly interested in long term commitments.

And the thread that binds them all together? Expediency. Have we gotten so busy that we are too busy to go out and meet someone, or are we afraid to go out? "The bar scene doesn't work for me". "I only want to marry a Christian." Self-selection becomes obsolete. Marry a number.

I'd rather play Spin the Bottle and hope for a winner.

Treadmills

I hate treadmills. I have one now. I have had many. I have had gym memberships so I could use a treadmill. It's the bane of my existence.

Years ago, I ordered an inexpensive treadmill. Why was it inexpensive? Because it was in beta testing. Who knew there was such a thing? But dayum – I'm in! So hubby and I pushed and pulled that really heavy box up a flight of steps and he put it together in our bedroom. I was so excited! It had lots of bells and whistles, and really nice cupholders. [Editors note: I have a thing for cupholders. Deal with it]

The next morning, I leap out of bed, ready to take on the treadmill. TV on – check. I'm ready to watch the news and do my treadmill thing. Safety drills had been done the night before, and mechanical checks were thorough. I was ready to rock.

For some reason, I thought it was okay to get on the treadmill (since it was mine, and I was at home) in socks and my pajamas. It's not the best idea, but I'm sure there are people out there who have done worse. So there I am, trucking along, at a blistering 2.0 walk, in my socks and pajamas.

Hubby is sitting on the edge of the bed putting on his socks and we're talking about whatever it was we talked about when we actually talked to each other. And then ... it happened.

For reasons unknown to me, except to serve as a jarring reminder of my incredible stupidity, the treadmill races off, of its own accord, to 10 mph. Now. A 50+ year old woman who cannot rub her stomach and pat her head at the same time, in her pajamas (specifically a Lanz flannel nightgown) and socks is probably not going to handle this situation with aplomb.

For a fat girl, I flew pretty far.

Hubby was in the unenviable position of having witnessed this first hand. I mean, honestly. How do you stay alive in your marriage when you've just seen this? What do you say that is not going to get you banned to the couch for the remainder of your married life?

He said nothing. At all. Just finished putting on his shoes and tied them. Asked if I was all right and headed off to work. He probably needed a Depends for the ride into work.

Long story short. I didn't break anything and I returned the treadmill. And then I joined the gym so that at least I would have tennis shoes on the next time I crashed and burned.

Flash forward to the present. Okay not the exact present, several months ago. Still huffing and puffing with the gym membership. I've actually put the treadmill to use and have run a couple of 5ks. Well, okay "run" may not be the most descriptive word. But still. Not too shabby for someone whose initial training started out at 2.0 mph.

So, one evening I take myself down to the gym and position myself on the middle of three treadmills. Yes. Three. It's a very small gym in a very small town. I'm so good at this treadmill thing now that I don't bother with the emergency key. Like everyone else who runs on a treadmill at the gym, I run with the key plugged in and wound around the bar, just dangling. I guess if you were "going down" or "listing", you could pull the key and the treadmill would stop. Not this girl. I don't need no stinking key.

So this night, I am just running along, normal snail pace (not really, I was running about a 9 minute mile at this time), and all of a sudden, my treadmills stops, and the screen starts flashing red, saying "EMERGENCY!" "EMERGENCY!" The sudden stop has now made my neck snap like a rubber band, and I have absolutely no clue as to what is going on. … I am like .. where? Where is the emergency? Is the gym on fire? And then I look down and see that somehow the emergency key has dislodged.

Now. You may not know me personally, but I am 59 years old with white hair. Not a skinny minny or a coordinated chick. I am old and fat. And I cannot figure out how to put this key back in the machine to make the screen stop flashing red. It didn't detach from the key part, the whole thing came out somehow.

The odd thing about it all was that, well, as much as I hate to admit this, no one cared. I felt like I should be being showered in riches, the damn thing sounded like a slot machine. I guess the peeps on either side of me could see that I was okay .. confused, but okay .. and apparently the key didn't set off any alarms to gym management that a fat old lady might have fallen off the treadmill. Clearly their liability insurance premium was paid.

I did finally figure it out, it was a USB issue. And I finished my run. But, since one of the points of my gym membership was the safety of not exercising alone in the event of a "situation", I decided to buy a treadmill and subscribe to Life Alert. Cheaper but stupid looking.

Damn skippy. I got this.

THE Plan

I made the comment when 2014 rang itself in that I was oh so grateful to have 2013 in the rear view mirror. It wasn't a stellar year for me. Not necessary to get into all the things that made it so unhappy, except to say that all of the issues resolved. Not to my liking in some cases. Which is why I blamed 2013 for screwing up my life. Just like 2012. And 2011 .. well, you get the drift.

A wise and wonderful friend said to me not long ago - why are you blaming the year for that which was inevitable under the Plan. Why aren't you celebrating the lessons learned. Hmmm.

[Potential spiritual bullshit call by some. SPOILER]

The Plan, as I call it, is the plan I believe we lay out for ourselves in advance of coming around again in life. I know that not everyone accepts that theory, hell .. we can't all agree on the concept of a higher power, and what to call it. I call it God, and I accept that fully. I believe that we are all a part of God, all working toward a common good, all here to be our highest and best. I believe that we have charted our destiny before arriving, and that some of us make choices that will, inevitably, hurt or cause pain to others. But I now believe that even that is known to us before we arrive via Mom. The question is: how do we choose to handle the pain? Do we bury it inside and let it eat at us? Do we carry it as a red badge of courage, hoping others will admire our courage and fortitude, when in reality, we are looking for pity? Do we simply accept it and move on?

I think we have to stay in touch with it, and while saying we should "embrace" pain or unhappiness or loss sounds pretty Pollyanna, I do think that is the answer. Ignoring these things will not make them go away, and ignoring them defeats the purpose

35

of learning from them. And isn't learning the exact reason we exist? I think so.

So, I took my friend's advice, and I went back and looked at last year. I endured more physical pain than I thought I possibly could with eye surgery. Yes. I lost my sight, but it was regained. Yes it was painful. But I will never, ever take my sight for granted again. A win.

I lost someone to cancer that I loved more than I can ever describe. I felt like I'd been screwed out of a possible second chance, even though that in and of itself was most unlikely. Pretty selfish on the whole, don't you think? This person faced his death with more dignity than I faced learning about his death. There's a lesson there. We are going to lose those we love. And we are going to die. It's really that simple. And I believe with all my heart that we go on (ALL of us) to a better place. So, it's just selfish to see things any differently. I will miss him for the rest of my life, there is no question about it. We shared something special. That is never gone. That is what I take from it all.

So, these are my thoughts in the rear view mirror. Adele, you were absolutely correct my dear friend. It's not about what we lose. It's about what we gain through loss. It's just so damn hard to sort that out sometimes.

Are you my Daddy?

A friend of mine has a young daughter, like pre-k age. Tonight, my friend is attempting to explain the somewhat abstract concept to her daughter that seahorse daddys carry babies in their tummys, not seahorse mommys. What??? I was still eating dirt at her age.

Because I was so incredulous (and quit looking down your nose at me as if you already knew this. You know you didn't), I was provided an illustrated link tutorial. On my newest knowledge acquisition, I make the following observations:

1. Without further study, I cannot determine the difference in seahorse gender unless one is in the family way.

2. I'll never really understand this whole mating without appendages thing. Fish, slugs, you know. And the poor T-Rex. So close, but so far away. I don't believe that whole asteroid extinction theory. I think they just gave up from sexual frustration.

3. One of the pregnant male [OXYMORON ALERT] seahorse facts I learned tonight is that the baby seahorse gestational period is short. Moreover, Mr. Mom can become pregnant quite soon after delivery.

Now. My entire point here is that the more different things are, the more they stay the same. Or, maybe it's just that huge "hahahahahahahaha" female mammals feel knowing this. The smugness felt knowing that "that guy is just the neighborhood bicycle, isn't he?" Do seahorses get headaches? Or the old standard "not tonight honey, I'm so tired from bearing 200 children - I need a break". Does Ms. Seahorse sigh heavily and head out for the neighborhood pub?

It's really mind boggling. It was easier understanding what happened to T-Rex. We can understand that.

I'm not at all adverse to role reversals. This one just struck me as funny.

Swim and procreate dude! Right on.

Revisiting the Should

I've got the flu, or some other ickiness that isn't fatal, but makes you want to shake your fist at the heavens and say "As God is my witness, I'll never throw up again!!" (sans radish, of course) ... I'll be going to the doctor shortly, but will be told that there is little anyone can do anymore with these stupid bugs except let them run their course. Just awesome. Another couple of days of not feeling it.

If you remember, I visited the idea of "shoulds" versus "wants" not too long ago. I want to free myself from the "shoulds" and concentrate on the "wants". I decided at that time that shoulds are self-imposed demands that society places on us. I inferred that this was not a good thing. I got hammered by readers on that. I want to revisit this.

To me "shoulds" are obligations, standards that are received. processed, and accepted by us based on our own moral code, wishes, wants, and desires. So "shoulds" can be selfish in and of their very nature. For instance, yesterday (despite feeling like left over cat poop), I felt like I "should" go to the gym and run. After all, I'd just bought a new Fuel Band (my old one fell apart) and hubby had just bought me new running shoes. Plus, I was eating crazy because I didn't feel well. Seriously. Those were my reasons. You see my point here, I'm sure. That was sooooo far from a legitimate "should" that it's almost ludicrous to include it in the same sentence.

That was a pure and simple "want". I wanted to assuage my own self-imposed guilt. A deception! I made myself feel guilty when, in fact, there was not enough money or guilt in the world to make me go get on a treadmill against my will. But, I was happy to blame the guilt on the externals - the money spent recently to help me with my running goals - rather than my ego.

I find that separating "should" and "want" is coming down to definition of the motivation, which in and of itself is selfish, yes? So, are there really "shoulds" in our existence, or are "shoulds" simply mechanisms we hide behind so that we appear to be morally righteous and upright in our actions? Hmmm.

Since this is still difficult for me to wrap my brain around, I'll take some easy ones:

I should call my daughter because I haven't spoken to her since last week = I want to talk to my daughter. The "should" suggests that either or both of us are under some kind of moral obligation to make a call. How incredibly self-absorbed is that? Do I worry that she is okay, I do. But she is an adult. If she wants me to know things, she will tell me.

I should attend a meeting at night for an organization I joined. I haven't been in a month. = I don't want to drive all that way on a cold, dark night for an hour and half, and spend my gas although it is an organization that I cherish. Now. Perhaps I should rethink my commitment to the organization if I feel this way. Regardless, this is not an expectation put on me by anyone other than myself. It could be argued, of course, that people in the organization depend on me, thus making it a "should", but that can only be the case if I "want" to put myself in that position.

So, I am now leaning toward the theory that there really are very few, if any, shoulds in the world. That shoulds are self-imposed wants that don't want to take responsibility for themselves. And that if we struggle against a should, perhaps it's because it's we need to be honest with ourselves.

I'm now going to eat myself alive inside trying to come up with ONE legitimate should to make myself feel better. *sigh* .. I really don't want to do that.

Fifty years ago this weekend. The birth of Beatlemania. My friend Scott sent me an incredible email today revisiting all the wonders of the Beatles. First recorded feedback, first this, first that. Each individual accomplishment by these four young men from less than fortunate backgrounds ... I don't know that there is a greater success story. And through all the changes, through all the innovations, each of the four remained true to themselves. Paul, the perfectionist. John, the cynic. George, the dreamer. Ringo, the Beatle. But as a whole - they changed everything that the world knew and believed in. John's "more popular than Jesus" comment, or his "those in the rich seats, just rattle your jewelry" .. intellect coupled with biting observation. Paul, always smiling. I always picture him singing "She Loves You", shaking his "do" and smiling. I would have sold a kidney to marry him.

George, the most spiritual of the group. Also, the one most maligned by John and Paul. It wasn't until his breakout on Abbey Road that he was recognized by critics, which is patently absurd in that were it not for the Harrison riffs, the Beatles would never have had the "Beatle" sound. And Ringo. The replacement for Pete Best. Luckiest moment of his life. Ringo was the not the best or most innovative drummer ever, but he was the perfect "back man" for the handsome leading men. The foil. Being a Beatle was his job.

So, those born from the late 40s and growing up during the 60's and 70's, can we agree that there is at least ONE Beatle song that underscored something incredibly memorable in your life? I have always acknowledged that the Beatles wrote the soundtrack of my life. And don't misunderstand. I loved the entire British invasion, and then groped my way through mind bending San Francisco acid music, and onward to what is now "classic rock": Aerosmith, etc. Man, I loved those huge ass headphones. They rock. Now we have ... "ear buds" or Dre Beats. Whatevah.

Nothing like hearing Pink Floyd with those big ass headphones on.

But I digress. This is my thank you to John, Paul, George, and Ringo. You gave me so much. You gave me happy music. You gave me harmony to die for. You gave me ditties that made absolutely no sense. You gave me concept albums that I had to consider tripping to so I could understand it as a whole, not just a collection of songs. You gave me the rooftop concert, and then, finally, you gave me Let it Be and the Long and Winding Road. I went from fourth grade through my senior year, when the Beatles finally called it a day. Unbelievable timing. But timeless and precious.

I married two men who played in Beatle tribute bands. One as Ringo, one as George. I eulogized my Ringo to the strains of "Across the Universe" and "I'll Follow the Sun". I have sobbed uncontrollably to "Yesterday". I have rolled down the car windows (yes, when you actually rolled them down) to sing "She Loves You" and "I Want to Hold Your Hand". I mourned a lost love to "I Will". And I shocked the living crap out of my parents in 9th grade by blasting "Why Don't We Do It In The Road" with my bedroom windows open. Oh. The horror.

Can anyone identify with the defilement of human life now represented by "Helter Skelter"? Or what the hell is "Norwegian Wood" about? And, one of my proudest achievements ever: learning to play "A Day in the Life" on the piano by ear.

I know that there are other bands, other songs we have fallen in love to, or hated. Probably every bit as memorable as the Beatles songs, but I don't think there is anyone over 50 who wasn't glad to be a part of it, and every musician under 50 owes the Beatles a huge debt.

Because you know .. they were right. All you need IS love.

Salad

Here is one of those stories that I'm not particularly proud of, but .. it happened. Not a lot of people know that I was married when I was 19. It didn't last long, and I'll probably talk about it again. But suffice to say, I made the decision to marry based on all the wrong reasons. In retrospect, it was about as big a mistake as you can make and survive. But, at the time, I was incapable of understanding the situation I had dug myself into.

My "then hubby" and I, both youngsters (19 and 21) were quite spoiled, but I think we were genuinely good people who gravitated to each other because of the fear and self-loathing of being alone. Sounds pretty heavy duty for such a young age, but I think that's a fairly accurate statement. He was not a bad person, nor was I. We were just far too young and immature to have taken this rather drastic and legal step.

One weekend, one of my closest friends from home came down to visit us. Jim and I had been friends literally since diapers, and he had even been selected by my groom to be in the wedding party. Our friendship was based on nothing more than just that – friendship. I remember one time in high school, we were both in single mode, and we tried to kiss. We had had a lot to drink, and we ended up outside together, throwing up next to each other. Way more comfortable vomiting together than making out. Maybe not the most romantic story here, but certainly illustrative of the relationship.

So, Jim comes down to visit us, and "then hubby" decides we should have a great party to celebrate! Right on. I loved parties. It was a great success! Everyone came out for it. Much beer, alcohol, and weed was consumed. If you know me, you know that I can be a bit of a light weight sometimes. Okay, most of the time. So, somewhere during the evening, I decided I needed to go upstairs and lie down.

Now, here is the totally inexplicable decision I made. To this day I can't defend it. I think I thought I would just lie down for a minute and then head back downstairs. I laid down on the bed, fully clothed (and just to make you laugh, I had on my shoes: a pair of saddle shoes. Don't hate!), with my head at the foot of the bed.

But here's the thing. I didn't go into our room to lie down, I went into the guest room and laid down on one of the twin beds. Door open, lights on .. the whole 9 yards. I really think I meant to just nap and then rejoin the crowd. Why I chose that room, I will never know. So, at some point, Jim comes upstairs to go to bed. Lo and behold Goldilocks snoring and drooling on the other bed. Jim probably wasn't in the best shape either, so down he went on the other bed. Fully clothed, lights on.

"Then hubby" and I had a cat. She was totally spoiled. For some reason, at some point, I awakened, was aware of the cat and as I would have done were I asleep in my own bed, I got up, put her out of the room and shut the door. Went straight back to where I was, laid down and out like Cassius Clay got me with an uppercut. Anyone else been there?

Not a good move.

[NSFW language coming] When I woke up the next morning, I almost shit my pants. Here I was – still fully dressed and on top of a made bed – my best male friend ever sleeping in the other bed and .. the door is shut. This was not going to turn out well. There was not a doubt in my mind.

"Then hubby" had obviously slept in our bed, but he was nowhere to be found. I immediately awakened Jim and the problem became obvious to him as well. And again, sometimes you just can't believe how foolish you can be, or why you don't make better choices.

For some insane reason, instead of getting in our cars and leaving, we both decided that it made more sense to stay and defend our honor. WTF is that? Probably admirable thinking on the honor side of it, but holy crap. These folks I hung with were armed in 1974.

So, expecting death, and to make it more tolerable, Jim shared with me a couple of the Seconals he had tucked into the lining of his suitcase. If you don't know what they are, look them up. I had two and he had two. We chased them with Jack Daniels, and smoked some weed. I was feeling pretty damn invincible. We had both accepted that we were dead peeps walking, and frankly were okay with it given our state of selves at that moment.

Until my mother-in-law called. Didn't see this one coming folks. I made Jim answer the phone (dinosaur days, before caller ID) because I was pretty much glued into place on the couch by this point. Apparently she told him that we would need to come over and meet them at their house, that "then hubby" was there, and the whole family would be going out for dinner.

I'm not sure it doesn't get any more bizarre than this, trust me. We think we're going to be killed and eaten by the family. My mother-in-law had a monkey. Seriously. And guns. Jim and I debated the whole mission. We seriously were so past the logic place that we got dressed and drove over. This is where my memory gets a little dodgy. Fear will do that to you.

"Then hubby" was there, glaring at me. I couldn't do much but giggle. Seconal, weed, and Jack will do that to you. We all pile into cars and head out for the local steakhouse. I vacillated between tears and laughter. I don't remember much more than that. We get to the steakhouse and waited while they put tables together. Yes. There were five children, and several of them had significant others. So this was a good sized group. When the tables were ready, Jim and I were instructed to go to the seats at the end, next to the wall, across from each other. "Then hubby" sat next to me. I remember very little else about the seating arrangement.

I do remember that every time I looked across the table, I burst out laughing. It was amazing … laughing in the face of death. But Seconal and Jack will give you an incredibly stupid sense of boldness.

We ordered, and headed for the salad bar. In this particular restaurant, the salad bar was round. That was not a good thing for us. We needed boundaries. I don't know if you recognize the feeling of having to try to act like you're not a mess, but I can tell you .. it's damn tough. Especially under those type of conditions.

But, the other spectacular thing about being that messed up is … you can't predict what's gonna happen. You are just in the moment. Perception of time and space is a problem. So, around and around and around and around the salad bar Jim and I go. My god, it was endless! I couldn't wrap my brain around the enormity of it. We walked and giggled, walked and giggled.

As I go to put some 1000 Island dressing on my salad and glance to my left just in time to see Jim go face first into the bowl of mixed iceberg lettuce.

Oh.
My.
God.

And I look down at my bowl, and there are three pieces of lettuce, drowning in 9 cups of 1000 Island dressing. And Jim's head is in the lettuce. I'm thinking he might even be asleep. Well, this won't work at all. I'm not going through this shit by myself. After all, this was all HIS idea. So I pull his head up out of the lettuce bowl, and dust him off. The little pieces of carrot were the most difficult really.

On top of this, I am laughing so hard, I might have wet my pants. All in all, just about the funniest thing I've ever seen, bar none! Meanwhile ... "the" table and the rest of the restaurant are not amused. At all. We were escorted back to our seats, where we sat quite numbly for the rest of the meal. I still laughed when I looked across the table, so I made myself stare at my plate. The ire from "then hubby" was palpable. I just knew I was going to be a dead woman soon. So, I had dessert. Just in case.

As it turned out, "then hubby" accepted the story as the truth it was, and even got a slight chuckle out of our behavior in the restaurant. To be fair, it's not as though he was without his own vices and drama. The marriage didn't work out very well, but ... it was a bang up weekend of memories.

Kinda.

Still can't eat 1000 Island dressing to this day without fear.

Don't even want to tell you how monkeys make me feel.

Emily

At the suggestion of a friend, I am reading Emily Dickinson now. I can recall a time when, in a literature class, that would have been tantamount to a death sentence. I hated poetry. I hated Chaucer; I hated anything that didn't readily scream out the answers that the teacher wanted to hear. So, I did what was required (which probably included Cliffs Notes) and moved on through my education, not realizing the voices I'd so casually blown off in youth would resonate so strongly in a mature mind.

First, I need to apologize to those earnest teachers who tried so valiantly to bring us into contact with classics. It was the 70s, and quite frankly, if it didn't have mechanical feedback attached to it in some way or dancing multi-colored ducks, we weren't listening. Well, most of us weren't listening. OKAY maybe just some of us. But I wasn't. Except for Dickens. Mary Corr taught my 11th grade English class, and we read Dickens. Perhaps it was because I had seen the Alistair Crowley version of "A Christmas Carol" that allowed me to look inside a classic. After all, I'd "seen" it, right? I could visualize *someone else's* idea of Dickens. Everything I ever read that Dickens wrote was based on that horrible, scary version of Scrooge. Someone else's vision.

In 9th grade, I attended (under duress) a very prestigious private girls school in New Jersey. (I can HEAR you laughing people!) I hated it. I was in 9C English, which I guess means I fell somewhere around average on the intelligence scale. My teacher seemed ancient, Miss Hope Corken. She assigned 9C Shakespeare's assignment: "As You Like It." Every other 9 class got "Romeo and Juliet". Seriously? The average kids can't handle it? The other classes got field trips into NYC to go see de Laurentis's new movie. Not 9C. We struggled along with Rosalind pretending to be a guy and hanging out with Robin Hood while the other classes got naked Leonard Whiting. It bears repeating that Miss Corken only taught one section of 9 English. And only I could have pulled that short straw. However, after seeing "Romeo and Juliet", through someone else's vision, I colored my perception of Shakespeare's crew as pretty hip peeps. Cool clothes too.

But I digress. The classics, in MY life, were always brought to me courtesy of Proctor and Gamble. Or some other commercial promoter. My generation never really read the classics, as much as we saw the classics. And the problem with that is that no version of any tale or poem is the way you should see it. Each of us needs to see and hear with our own eyes and ears to feel the papyrus that Socrates wrote on, or the scraps of envelopes that Dickinson jotted on, or visualize and hear the twelve men of the jury. To feel the dust rise up in Steinbeck and Cather. To feel the grittiness of a jail cell through Capote. But unless we embrace a time trodden tradition of actually taking the time to sit down and read something (and yes, you can use your Nook or Kindle or other Ereader) .. we are only allowing ourselves to be exposed to a fraction of the picture. We see things through another's lenses, not our own.

So, I have started on Dickinson. Why? Because someone I hold in high regard suggested that I take a look at her, that I might find myself in some of what she felt. I panicked. I will be frank with you. Here was someone urging me to dive into classical poetry, a person who taught the subject, who wrote dissertations that were above the heads of professors. Good grief, what if I really WAS 9C, and couldn't grasp the concepts of Dickinson. What if I couldn't hold a mutually reciprocal scholarly conversation about her writing?

He laughed at me. And he said, just read it. Don't try to understand things. Just feel it.

And that is where I think we, as a whole, have lost our way. We are technologically advanced, we can do the most amazing things simply by pressing a button. But we have robbed ourselves of the pleasure and knowledge of the past by reducing it to a place of little consequence. Names only. No indepth study. We've got Wiki. We've got the press of a button. Knowledge in an instant.

Knowledge, but not understanding. Knowledge but not enjoyment.

I'm going to take my time with this chick Dickinson. I'm liking her way of thinking. I'm also thinking that the guy who recommended this to me is pretty damn smart.

My Diane

Time to celebrate the life of someone very few of you had the opportunity to meet (if any). Most know that I grew up in the town of Chestertown, on Maryland's Eastern Shore. Chestertown is a beautiful place, the entire Eastern Shore is a beautiful place. It has its areas of history, bucolic scenery, ocean, bay, blue crabs, beer ... wait. It's getting away from me. But mostly, it is a place of community. I had the good fortune of growing up there in the mid-50s and 60's.

For those too young to recall, that was a time of social change and racial equality. It was also the time of June and Ward Cleaver family living. I'm talking about the ability to play outside until dark without fear of abduction. I'm talking about a slower paced way of life. Of there not really being haves and have nots, but desperate school rivalries between Rock Hall, Galena, and Chestertown. Bonfires, ice skating, touch football, Church League basketball. All very "just a few steps" behind the chaos of the 60s. Not that we were unaware on any level, I recall when we integrated the all black Garnett School (grades 1-12) with Chestertown Elementary and High Schools. I was in 7th grade and totally was trying to understand why this had not been done before. But even as my liberalism would become more defined as I aged - I just thought having black kids in our class was the right thing. But, even now I look back at that and realize that there was a certain caste system even then. I was in Class 7A. We had two black students in our class. 7E a much larger proportion. I never really thought about the disproportionate nature of it all until I was older. Then it made me sick to my stomach.

I preface this post with this historical reference so you can attempt to frame the world I grew up in. Slow paced, faith based, All American and just as screwed up behind closed doors as you'd ever want to think about. Only we didn't know at the time. So on we went.

53

In 1967, my Dad owned a small chemical company in Chestertown (Lehigh Chemical). They manufactured a lubricant that NASA used. Obviously it was a cash cow at that time, so my Dad sold his company to Tenneco Oil, then based in Houston. I love my Dad with all my heart, but for as much as he knew bottom lines and staying in the black, he didn't always make good choices with respect to his business fortunes.

As a result of the buyout, Dad was made a Vice President (which I now know means little to nothing in the corporate world) and we needed to move from Chestertown to Houston. I was devasted. I was just wrapping up my 7th grade year, and used to tire swings and lazy summers at the Club pool and dock on the river. So, in June of 1967, the Haacke family packed it up (after a goodbye party at Dee Willis's house in Chesmar), and off we flew to Houston, Texas.

Now. If you're familiar with the 60s at all, you know that by 1967, the times they were a changing. I just didn't realize how much or how fast. Let's put it this way. I got on the plane in Baltimore with a skirt just below my knees, very 50s poodlish. By the time we landed in Houston several hours later, fashion dictated hem lengths of just below your butt. This was not good. Not good at all.

I don't know how many remember their 8th grade year at all, let alone in such excrutiating detail as I do (can't remember where I put my purse now, but I know I went to Spring Valley Junior High) .. but let me put it this way: 8th grade is NOT a time when you want to be the odd girl out. Your hormones are starting to jump around, popularity is an issue, as is acne, and when your mother (country born and bred) doesn't want to go with the social flow of a new place .. well, you look stupid and you're ostracized. I know that I'm not the only person who ever felt that way, I get it. My own sister, who was then in 4th grade, was so unhappy that she would go out the back door to walk to school, and Mom would find her sitting on the front steps an hour later. She hated it. I hated it. But still, I was strangely fascinated with this new breed of girls who had stick straight blonde hair down their back, short dresses with neon fishnet tights, patent leather heeled Mary Janes and matching purses. Let's not forget the British invasion of cosmetics like LOVE products, which included the mandatory pale pale PALE pink lipstick.

So there I was. Already tall, already starting to "mature", dark haired (though straight, no ironing required) and a mutant among my 8th grade peers. It was a drag, I am not going to lie to you. I don't think there is much more painful than being the ugly newbie. Cruelty magnified. I was miserable. I tried every conceivable ploy with my Mom so that she would let me update my wardrobe, but that wasn't happening. I'm a fighter, but there is only so much control one has at that point in their life. I came from Chestertown, and by God, I would stay in the 50s.

Then a miracle occurred. A young couple in their late 20s moved in across the street from us. Pete and Diane Tennant. Pete was a young attorney, and Diane his beautiful wife (and I mean in the classic blonde petite beauty sense with big Texas hair, which was okay at that time). My parents fell in love with them and vice versa, even though there was an age difference. When I met Diane, I knew on some level, that I'd been saved. She was an angel come to earth for me.

Diane was roughly 12-13 years older than me but younger in heart and spirit than anyone I'd ever known. She absolutely glowed with love. I thought she was the most perfect creation God had ever made. She loved me, and I loved her. Finally I had a big sister, someone who actually cared and would listen to me. Could feel my pain in being ostracized. Ran interference with my Mom.

Because Mom loved Diane so much, she was finally able to understand what was happening with me. Sometimes it takes an objective third party to intervene. Mom went kicking and screaming into 1968, but changes were made, I was made a little more hip, my confidence increased a little, and I reached out and made friends. Mom and Dad spent tons of time with Diane and Pete and their friends, so it was all around a match made in heaven.

Diane hosted my birthday sleepover (which, by the way, was well attended) and she took me shopping. I actually snared a boyfriend (who was adorable, Rick) who gave me his ID bracelet. Pre-engagement type thing ;) The music was wonderful - we were moving into Sgt. Pepper and the Monkees, and I was a happy girl.

Until late spring in 1968 when Dad announced he'd been transferred back east, this time to New York. Oh shit. What can you say? I was heartbroken. Mom was heartbroken. Diane was heartbroken. But how do you change fate? You don't. You roll with it. And I still remember the picture taken of me going up the steps of the plane (that was when you still walked the tarmac). I had on a little black and white polka dot dress with white patent pumps and matching purse. I gave Rick back his ID bracelet. I didn't feel like I could tie him down at that point (and yes, I truly believed that! LOL!).

Long story short, I was enrolled in Kent Place School where uniforms were required (much to my mother's happiness), and at the end of 9th grade, Dad retired and we moved back to Chestertown where time away had allowed the Shore to catch up with fashion trends. Dad insisted I attend private school (Gunston), I said I'd run away. We were at a stalemate.

I called Diane and whined about the plans for my future incarceration. Diane flew me down to Ft. Worth, where they are now living, and spent endless hours on the phone "negotiating" with my Dad. If you know him, you know he loved and believed in her because when I came home, I came home with suitcases full of clothes for public school. And so it went.

Pete and Diane visited often, and they soon had a beautiful daughter of their own. Nothing slowed Diane down, she just incorporated that little girl into everything. When I was 21, my Mom had major surgery. Major. Diane flew up to stay with Dad and I (my sisters were in private school in Baltimore). It was nerve wracking and difficult. But Mom pulled through.

On the day that Diane was to fly back to Ft. Worth, she came to the hospital to say goodbye to Mom. My mother was medicated, to say the least. My sister had a tie dye long sleeve shirt on in purple/green and Mom asked her where she had gotten all those bruses. So, needless to say, Mom was on a planet that we didn't share.

When Diane sat next to her on the bed, Mom started crying. Diane said "Kay, whatever are you crying about?" and Mom said "I am never going to see you again." Diane threw back her head and laughed her beautiful laugh, and kissed Mom on the cheek and said "Kay, your operation is over and you're fine. Don't say silly things." And with a flurry of Givenchy perfume, waves, hugs and kisses, she was gone.

In August of that year, I was preparing for my good friend Kevin's wedding and looking forward to him and Mary tying the knot that weekend. I was working for a veterinary hospital in Queenstown, and so had come home from work and was lying down for a bit before a date that night. My boyfriend, Gene, called, and as I walked through the family room to the kitchen, something seemed not right. And indeed, as I passed her, my youngest sister said "Oh by the way, Diane died today".

What? I never even had grandparents so except for a couple of friends killed in teen driving accidents, I didn't even know what that meant. I mean. Yes, they were gone, but I hadn't loved them, not like this. This was pain I'd never even thought possible (little did I know then that it was pain I would experience many times, this was just the first event). Of course, my parents were inconsolable. They made immediate plans to fly to Ft. Worth that weekend - the weekend of Kevin and Mary's wedding. I would not be going to Ft. Worth. I'm still not sure if that was a good thing or not.

Diane had been sitting in her best friend's kitchen, on the floor, planning a party. I can still see her to this day - that was not an unusual pose for her. She was, although quite wealthy, one of the least pretentious people I've ever met. They were planning a Mexican fiesta for the weekend - this was Diane's forte. Bringing people together, having fun, being happy. She looked at her friend, said "my head hurts", and died of a cerebral hemmorage before the ambulance could arrive.

She had saved my life, and now she was gone. Just like that. I would never hear her voice or see her beautiful, most precious face ever again. It is impossible for me to describe her gentleness, her kindness, her beauty because I don't have the words. Tears run down my face now, thirty five years later, remembering her love. Her genuine caring. I thought of her precious little daughter who would never know what I, a stranger, had known of her mother and her goodness. If I thought that life was unfair before that moment, I knew in an instant that it would never be fair or right or as bright and loving as it had been.

Pete ended up drinking himself into the grave, leaving their daughter to be raised by Diane's mother and father, whom I loved equally. I always wondered how they could bear it. Diane was their only child, but having their granddaughter (now married with a daughter of her own) had to be equal parts pain and pleasure.

If ever there were anyone I would want to be when I grew up, it was Diane. She was kind, compassionate, engaging, lively, caring, ... just ... caring. She saved my life. There is no doubt in my mind. I loved her deeply, I miss her every single day of my life, and

I know that she is an angel watching over me. I just wish .. oh I just wish .. I could get one more hug.

Valentine's Day

Ahhh Valentine's Day!

Romantic love ... That's what this holiday is about. Hugs and kisses and roses and chocolates. Promises that frame a future. Beginnings.

I don't much care for this holiday, to be honest. For me, it began in elementary school with the collection of valentines in your class. Oh, I hope Stevie sent me one. Woe to the 3rd grader whose valentine collection bag wasn't as full as another's. Really what it meant to me was that x number of valentines correlated to your place on the popularity scale. A hateful measurement really, but I'd wager few women of today would dispute this humble beginning of the "OMG!!! Genie got so many more valentines than me. She's so smart and pretty, and I'm so fat and stupid and weird." Tell me how many were immune from the self-deprecation wrought by penny valentines? Conversely, was there a greater high than receiving one from that special person in whom the sun rise and set, or the crushing aftermath of discovering that Shelley had received an identical card?

It seems ridiculous, this tradition. It's like a gigantic world wide mixer. Yes, the first flutters of infatuation are mind bending, but no box of candy can guarantee love. No card can confirm commitment. It's hard work. Love can leave you flat and restless, or over the moon happy. Mostly it's somewhere in between. It's steady, non-judgmental, patient, caring.

I suppose that, bottom line, I am annoyed over the triteness of the Valentines Day tradition. Love isn't a tradition you observe annually, it's very difficult agreement that people work through every day. It's the compromises that should be celebrated, the patience that evolves into a sense of security. Love is just so much more than a card or box of candy. Or a measurement of one's feelings which then can translate into self-worth (or lack thereof).

And yet, even as we age, we still revel in "look what my wonderful significant other did for me for Valentines Day. We hate each other pretty much the rest of the year, but as you can see, I still have a place in the popularity continuum." Why do you think peeps get all a flutter when they receive flowers on Valentines Day at work? Instagram will blow up too. Because we are proud that we deserve these flowers.

Folks, you don't need these accoutrements to know if you are loved. Some of us are, some of us aren't. Some of us care, some of us don't. Dumb Valentines Day doesn't define you as love worthy. The knowledge that you are happy, with or without a partner, is your box of candy.

That was almost Forrest Gumpy, wasn't it?

I'm revisiting the shoulds, kind of. I read a great blog yesterday that discussed the "shoulds" (I'm thinking that "should" may be the 2014 topic d'annee). The blog discussed shoulds as blocks to not listening to spiritual suggestions. In other words, when we throw up a should, it is because we don't want to listen to suggestions from our spiritual guides, mentors, angels, God .. however you want to view it. The blog suggested that we tend to ignore those types of interventions because they are uncomfortable for us.

I'm afraid of redundancy, but this seems to be such a critical sticking point for me, and for many others probably. I've read a lot about the definition of shoulds, and why we need to free ourselves from them (self-imposed limitations), *but nobody has been real specific as to how to do it.* I mean, do you just jump out there and say "screw the shoulds, screw my perception of responsibility", or is there some kind of middle ground?

The shoulds are self-imposed but based on how we perceive right and wrong. Those attributes we learned, adopted, and put into play in our lives. So, by discarding a should, are we saying to the world, but most importantly to ourselves, that we are doing something wrong?

I used to think that was the case. But I'm coming around to believe that our morals are already decided, static to some extent. But, and a huge but, how many times can you make a case for something you've done that you believe was wrong, but .. yet you can justify it. We've all done that. It's called lying. Not to anyone else, but to yourself.

That's where the honesty comes in, I think. It is so difficult to say "I wanted to do this and I did it. It might not have been something I thought I'd ever do, or would think correct, but it made me [happy/sad/peaceful/content/angry], and I can live with it."

There is not a person alive who wants to be judged by anyone. But we will judge ourselves - and quite harshly most of the time. So, why do we not accord ourselves the same respect we show to others? Judge not. That means yourself as well. That means discarding a should if you don't like it. You're allowed to do that.

We all go out on a limb (for the most part) not to hurt others, and we should not hurt others. Believe this: It is not okay to hurt yourself either. So, if a should hurts? It's not necessary for your life. Trust that.

And I'm gonna start doing that ... maybe tomorrow .. not sure what I should do .....

The Cardinal

It is snowing again ..now .. nowhere near what it has been snowing, but enough to be wintry looking and wet. Roads are fine. But damn if I'm not tired of it all. Yes Virginia, there is global warming.

I look out my bedroom window this morning and there perched on the railing is a cardinal. So incredibly vibrant red, little feet making snow tracks. Just beautiful. My first concern was for its health, but I read up on it and find that cardinals are 12 month birds. Now I don't think they'd do well in the arctic, of course, but they are hardy and harbingers of good luck. I felt pretty good about that. Because this was "my" bird. My time, my space, my bird. Think of what it takes for any winged creature that is not a bat to visit the residence of "she who has four cats that are always hungry." I figure that alone spoke to its intentions of being in my right space at the right time.

As we all do, I immediately googled to see if I stood on my right foot, tapping my left forefinger on my temple, and spinning in alternating circles, the visit of the cardinal would bring me good fortune in the form of so much money, I could use it to line the cat pans of the aforesaid four hungry cats. But, regretfully, no such ritual exists.

In fact, there really isn't much about cardinals with respect to spiritualism, except that they are fiery birds that portend good luck (again, if standing on your right foot, etc. etc. ... no, I kid). Cardinals are beautiful - and the state bird of more states than any other (including WV my WV friends!). The Cherokee believed that the cardinal was the daughter of the sun. If you saw it soaring toward the sun - good luck would come your way.

How extraordinary! That seeing that beautiful bird this morning tip toeing through the snow was a message. He came to tell me to believe in myself, that I can handle this, and to take pride in myself. That brings tears to my eyes.

Because really, we should all be able to communicate the message of the cardinal to ourselves. Who better to take pride in us, than us? Who better to believe in us, than us? I get that sometimes those who direct our steps sometimes feel that a refresher course is needed, and I think I understand why mine came today.

Betrayal

You expect something vitriolic, don't you? Not happening. The word itself is ugly enough. Worse though is that no one allows themselves to think they've done it; but, I'm willing to bet there is but only one of us who has ever walked this earth that hasn't done it.

I'm not sure it's okay to ever "do" this word. There are notable examples that don't bear retelling. But then there's the insidious daily/hourly incidents of which we are all guilty. And I say that, without removing myself from this generalization. 'Cause I am guilty of it. As a matter of fact, I can't find it in myself to NOT see Judas as a human being. He is a villain. Rotting in hell, right?

I think I might be on the Hell Express for thinking he might just have been doing what he thought needed to be done to take care of those he loved. As I see it, Judas is the only one who gets a pass on … betrayal. His was planned. Hell, look up the definition of betray and guess whose face you see? But were it not for his part in the plan, a lot of us would not have the faith that we have.

What I'm trying to piece together is how the betrayals made by me and received by me are part of any plan. They all hurt. They keep happening. As long as I trust, I either violate that trust or am violated by it. The alternative is to stop trusting. For me, that would be like not breathing. Even if you give me a reason, I probably will find a way to forgive (and maybe even do double emotional damage by making it my fault somehow).

So why then am I surprised when I am betrayed again? And should it concern me on some moral level that the shock and awe of the betrayal really is leveling out? Are people really all the same? I don't think everyone intentionally betrays. I think some make a practice out of it. And I get that it is their problem. And I know Don Miguel Ruiz would hold my palms over a flame because all of this violates the Four Agreements. Betrayal is not being impeccable with your word, it does not allow you to not take it personally, it causes you to make assumptions, and do your best is really up in the air as well. I know that argument can be made for this, I just don't have it.

I'm tired of taking it personally. But if I don't take it personally, would there be anyone whom I could exist with, or them with me? Do we settle for that comfortable spot where we accept that .. well .. it is what it is.

We can be so shallow. I say to myself and you, here and now: examine your motives.

Mom was right. If you can't say something nice, don't say anything at all. And I'd add, if you can't speak the truth (whatever your motives or problems are) ... then just don't speak. It hurts too many too much.

Crime and Chocolate

I so want Spring to be here. I am so tired of gray everywhere (except my hair, which I am loving!). Easter will be here next month. I hate Easter. I love Easter for the religious significance, but I'm not going there. I'm talking about the holiday Easter, with bunnies and eggs and chicks.

Easter fell on April 6 in 1958. How do I know this? It's burnt into my memory. It put into gear the process of my first attempted felony.

I was four. And truly adorable. I don't know what happened, so don't ask. I had skated through my first four years being coddled, greatly loved, and generally spoiled. I loved my life.

Now, I'd noticed changes over the few months preceding April 6, but nothing threatening. Mom and Dad had explained that I was going to have a sister or brother (this was the old days where the sex of your baby was actually a surprise), but honestly. I had no frame of reference and no reason to think it meant anything significant. Mom was blowing up like a balloon from the "baby in her tummy", but at four, unless it was in MY stomach, hey .... It's your life. I'm not judging.

Until Easter morning 1958.

Understand that absolutely nothing had given me reason to expect anything abnormal on this Easter morning. Nothing. What does a four year old know of labor and delivery? Eyes wide open – BINGO! It's Easter morning. Chocolate bunnies ahoy! Jump out of the bed, feet of the yellow one piece jammies hitting the brown rug, nothing to be seen but a splash of white rubbery material on the feet making a run for the chocolate. Out of my room, out into the hall, into the living room – charging for the front door where I am certain the golden cache of chocolate is waiting ....

Only to come to a screeching, sudden, life changing, maddening, and definitely unfair HALT. Something is terribly wrong! Oh no! There is no basket!!! Nothing, no faux chewed up carrot or rabbit turds. Nothing. At all. Including parents.

Natalie, my Mom's friend, was there though. Oblivious to my shock and immediate chocolate deprivation issues, she explained the Mommy and Daddy had gone to Baltimore to get my new baby sister who had been born that morning, and Happy Easter! What a big girl, aren't you so proud to have a new baby sister?

Frankly.

No.

WTF?

Chocolate – baby – chocolate – something I have no frame of reference for – chocolate – my parents aren't here and they didn't say goodbye – chocolate – Peeps

No. I'm not happy. Where is my Easter basket? Where is the chewed up carrot the Easter bunny left, and the raisin turds?

Natalie: "umm"

Me: that's what I thought.

And so began my short and insignificant life of crime. I don't even remember if the chocolate was ever made up, but I will never forget the homecoming. And every subsequent birthday celebration. I was NOT a good wingman. This kid had no neck and cried ALL THE FRIGGIN TIME. Good grief. Why did they have to screw up such a good thing. We were happy. I had ALL the presents. ALL the time, and I only cried a little bit. Now THIS? If you know me, you know that dealing with dissatisfaction is not a strong suit. So the only logical solution was to remove the issue. Hence my attempt to smother my sister with a pillow.

OBVIOUSLY I was not successful, and OBVIOUSLY I am not a psychopathic killer (I only binge eat, not kill) .. but to a four year old, it's really kind of a strategic reasoning. Eliminate that which comes between you and chocolate.

For the record. My mother was in the room when this happened, and it was less an attempt than a theory, but .. I was four. Keep in mind, also for the record, that I am adopted and I knew it. This was not just about chocolate (although mostly), but if getting a new sister was that easy, was it also not easy to return me?

I finally realized that I was not going to be returned, and eventually in July of 1960, yet another daughter joined the family. I still begrudged them birthday spotlight.

They had to SHARE a room, I got my own.

At this point in my life, I don't know if that was good or bad.

I really do not like Easter. I like the day after Easter, when the chocolate goes on sale.

Epiphany

I have to tell you ... I wish I was doing what I initially wanted to do with this book - write stories, journal a little bit, write up some of the funny stuff that happens - but I have (intentionally or otherwise) gone off track, and you are serving as unpaid therapists. Really wasn't my intention. I've gotten some incredible feedback from folks, all of which I've taken in, had appreciation for, and have thought about. I've come to some conclusions. Tell me what you think:

1. You never really know anyone except yourself. _And very very few of us are completely honest about that_. I'm not sure if it's because we're afraid of the truth, don't know the truth, or feel so psuedo-intellectual that we assume we know the truth. I got an email this morning where someone described themselves in three words. They were gritty and truthful and realistic. Of course, there is much more to this person, but he understands his reality, accepts it, and doesn't make it more (or less) than it is. I have so much respect for that.

So Epiphany #1: Know yourself. Completely, honestly, and without guilt. The more real you are about who you are, the more honest you are with the world.

2. Be kind to yourself. There are, of course, folks in this world who can't or won't accept responsibility for their actions. This renders them unable to be compassionate and to give back very little. To me, these are the arrogant, ignorant peeps. Then there are folks who accept responsibility for all actions in their world and carry overwhelming guilt and self-hate for things they had no control over. These are the martyrs. And then there are the very lucky folks who carry a balance .. they take responsibility for THEIR actions, but not for what they cannot control. I call them happy, balanced people. I do not fall into this latter

73

category, I am a martyr. I'm not entirely sure why, but I'm going to have a heart to heart with God and try to get it straight.

So Epiphany #2: Love yourself and check your ego at the door. Not everything is YOUR fault.

3. Believe in a Higher Power. God, Buddha, Allah, collective unconscious, Angels .. whatever you want to call it. We science until we die, but will science bring us around again? Or shape our souls? I don't think so. It chills me that in this world we have such extremes about this. Extremism causes hate. And the one thing that I do know is that God (using this word for the sake of unity of expression) hurts when we hate. And since he/she/it is responsible for that spark inside that drives you, that comforts you, that helps you know things that science can NOT explain, I'm calling us out on respect.

So Epiphany #3: Trust in a power greater than you. You (and I) are nothing more than the sum of many parts conceived and formed over more years than we can imagine. Not our weight or our height or our talent or our work ethic, our hearts and souls.

Now that I have pontificated, I will try to absorb this and change up my life a little bit. Sometimes, as I'm sure you do, I feel like I am constantly running on a hamster wheel, that there is no happiness, no future to look forward to. I am assured that this is not true. I'm banking on it now. I want you to bank on it too.

Once Upon a Dreadful Time

This is not a happy story. But it's one that I want to tell. The reason I want to tell it is because there is always a personal story behind statistics. I see so much information about this subject - stats that may or may not be correct, I don't know. But I read something today that made me want to come clean on this. Maybe by doing so, I can help others live with themselves in the face of overwhelming propaganda.

I believe in God. I believe that God and I had a bit of a chat before I entered this world, and sketched out how this was going to go. God gives us free will, but he doesn't always make the answers easy. And sometimes we make the wrong ones. But, that's what makes us human, and why we walk this earth.

So, today I read a Facebook comment about abortion- I am not 100% on the stat, but I think it said something like 500k per year, and the observation was that all those COULDN'T be rapes, so there you have it.

Well, abortions aren't all performed because of rapes, or incest, or any other unfortunate moral issue. And, I am not naive enough to believe that there are not those that use abortion as birth control - though I hope and pray that in the last decade we've been able to educate so that this is not so prevalent.

I am one of those statistics, so glibly quoted and judged. In 1971, pre Roe v. Wade, in my 16th year, I discovered I was pregnant. To be honest, and let me preface this with a plea NOT to judge my parents, I really had little idea how that happened. My Mom was not forthcoming with the birds and bees info, and in the 70s, we were just beginning to open up a bit in schools about the subject. Matters not really, what matters is that I became pregnant in April of 1971.

I tried denial. It worked for awhile. I knew that if it was true, life as I knew it would end. Forever. It was something I knew instinctively. Problem was. I had no clue where to go or what to do. In 1971, Planned Parenthood wasn't active in Kent or Queen Anne's County. Who could I ask? Certainly not my parents. My Dad had been diagnosed with heart disease and was headed for a bypass, which believe me, at that time, was a complete unknown. So ... if I were to tell him, what if he died? No, that wasn't an option. Plus, the whole idea of telling him scared the living bejesus out of me.

The father of my baby was a wonderful, wonderful person whom I loved very much. We were young, 16 and 17. And really kinda stupid about it all. We tried to get help from the Queen Anne's County Health Department, but they threatened to call our parents. It was quite the conundrum.

And so, weeks ticked by. I am not going to say I was an ostrich about it, but at 16, it's not something you really want to deal with. I know. I sound irresponsible. But that's how it was.

Finally, my mother "caught on", and told me I needed to give her a urine speciman for my annual summer check up. I smelled bullshit, and did the only thing I could do - add water to the speciman. Two days later, my mother picked me up and drove to me a private place in the country, pulled a calendar from under her car seat, said "I know you are pregnant, and I need to know when your last period was."

Well. There it was. Bingo. Trouble. Future. College. The horror of what will people say. All of that in those few words. I told her the best I could, and we drove home in silence. She said she was going to talk to our family doctor, but I was not to tell Dad (we didn't want him to die, after all).

The next day, I got a telephone call asking me to come down to Dad's office. This was not a big deal, I often helped him

76

out. But when I walked in the door, I knew this was not going to be a normal day. My mother, my father, and our doctor sat there and looked at me. My doctor explained that I was pregnant, that I was x weeks pregnant, and the options were limited. Remember, we are talking pre Roe v. Wade. My father said not a word. My mother and our doctor talked. I went home.

The next morning at breakfast, I was struggling through my bowl of cereal, and my Dad looked up from his bowl, and asked "Do you know the difference between a whore and a slut?". I said I did. He then asked me which one I was, and my world ended right then. Nothing, to this day, can alleviate that pain. I don't blame my Dad, and I don't want anyone else to do that either. I mean this. No judgment please on my parents. He loved me more than life. I cannot imagine the pain he felt, the betrayal. The fear. Was that a good thing to say? Nope. And as a parent, I would never do it. But, it's what happened, and no amount of trying to change it is going to work. This was the times.

So, in a nutshell, the decision was made to admit me to a hospital, under an assumed name. I was taken, admitted, and left sitting in a small waiting room. Finally, a nurse came to get me (I was a little confused on the name thing to be honest – I didn't get why I had to have a different name), and I was taken to an OR, a sheet draped high over my waist, and I got my first shot ever of an opiod. Good grief! I was little Miss Chatterbox, telling the assembled group, how sorry I was, how it was a mistake, how wonderful my boyfriend really was. We weren't horrible people.

He, of course, had been barred from any contact with me after the initial news came down. That changed, but that is a personal memory that I am not ready to share yet. But suffice to say that he saved my life. He challenged the decisions made, and confronted my father. He won the right to share this with me. Nothing would change the outcome, but at least we had each other.

So now, I am in a hospital in Baltimore, under an assumed name, having been dropped there by my boyfriend's stepdad and my mother. My father was in another Baltimore hospital, having had his surgery. I think my mother must have felt insane. I have had some kind of shot in my abdomen, and I am taken to a ward that was empty except for me and a girl named Nancy, from Norfolk. She had the most beautiful diamond ring. She was getting married soon. She didn't want to get married pregnant.

I figured I was finished - I had been told as much about this as I had about how to get pregnant, so I went to bed, expecting to wake up in the morning and go home. My water broke in the night - I thought I had wet the bed. So, I went down to bathroom, grabbed a bunch of towels and put them on top of the sheets. Not like the nurses ever responded to our ward.

The next morning, I was sitting next to Nancy's bed and we were watching TV. Her doctor came in (I never saw mine .. ever) .. and said her contractions should be starting soon, and he would be checking in. I was like ... OMG, you poor thing!!!!! I will stay with you and help you. You see, I thought I was done.

About noon it started. I don't need to describe labor and delivery. We all get it. Hours later I was taken to a small room on the maternity ward (how awesome to be in pain and in an elevator with normal people staring at you and then arriving at a place where EVERYONE was screaming. Talk about falling down the rabbit hole ....) Even at this point, I had no clue what was happening to my body.

I was settled into a bed in a room with just a sink and trash can, the white ones you step on to flip open? The pain was unbearable, unexpected and I have never been more frightened since. Finally blessed morphine. And more. And more. And then a weird feeling. My head was like a balloon (thank you Pink Floyd) but I felt compelled to sit up.

When I did, I saw there a perfectly formed little baby boy. He was dead. I was his mother. That was my moment of reckoning, of understanding the decisions that had been made for me, and which I, by not wanting to be one of "those" girls, had condoned. I screamed and screamed and screamed. I can still hear it in my mind.

My nurse came in, laid me back down, pushed on my tummy and when she was satisfied that all was finished, picked up the pad underneath me by the four corners, and walked to the trashcan, stepped on it to open it, and dropped my child into the trashcan.

I passed out cold. I woke up back in my room. Nancy was just being prepped to go up. I told her not to worry, I would be there for her. I had no clue what planet I was on. My brain had shut down.

When I woke up, Nancy wasn't back yet, but I wanted to go home. So desperately wanted to go home and try to process that which I have yet to process. I had a fever, they didn't want to release me. I put my thermometer in my water. I was released. I went to my boyfriend's home for a couple of days, and then I was flown to Cape Cod, where I "convalesced" for a month. I was not wanted at home.

This needed to go away, to be done with. It was over and done with and we all were expected to move on. On some level, I did. On most levels, I still cannot.

This was not a story of rape. Or incest. Or using abortion as birth control. This was a heart wrenching event that destroyed a family for many years. And even when the reconciliation came, it was bittersweet.

So, my point is this. To those are pro-life ... right on! I agree with you, every child is entitled to the best life possible. To those that are pro-choice, right on! The government cannot and should not try and legislate morality. But please .. both sides ... recognize that there are those who made that choice out of necessity, or even had that choice made for them, implicit consent or not. We carry scars you cannot possibly understand.

Past as the Future

So much to celebrate …. Some of those I love most are pregnant and due this fall (Alyson and Matt. I really wasn't kidding about the monogramming.) My "other" daughter, Lisa, ACED her Masters Degree (as I told her she would!!!). My bestie Kim made grandmother for the second time yesterday with the birth of grandson, Vincent, and my "Big Sis" Fran welcomed her first grandson today, Cole. Life is very good, and we are all really blessed!

I went "home" yesterday – to Chestertown, Maryland, where I was raised. I need to smell the Chesapeake Bay (preferably not when there are lots of dead fish, but there are times I'd take even that!), and I need to have my feet on the ground. It reminds me somewhat of "the red earth of Tara". I'll save Scarlett for another time, but the thing from which she drew her strength, her home, is the very thing from which I draw mine.

It was truly a beautiful blue sunny day. A little windy, but .. not so bad. I actually shot an 8 minute video of going across the Eastbound span of the Bay Bridge, so that I, as well as my fellow West Virginia runners, could get a sense of the length and incline of the Bridge. We will be running in the inaugural 10K Across the Bridge in November. I just know I'm going to lose it when the bridge starts swaying, but .. I'm going to do it and knock something else off my bucket list. Of course I need to edit the video because as I get closer and closer to the end of the Bridge and getting onto Eastern Shore soil, I get a little … nutty.

Chestertown has changed in many ways (who didn't want to tell me they closed the Tavern? Or that where Bud's Restaurant was is now a funeral home? Just wrong. I should have known about that!) but it's all cosmetic. The feeling is the same. The safety, the peace.

I visited a dear friend whom I hadn't seen in …. Probably 30 – 35 years. She is in assisted living in Rock Hall and it took her awhile to make connections to who I was. I was in a relationship with her son for a bit, and he died last summer. I was frightened of going – I didn't want to hurt her. I thought maybe I might remind her of her loss. But I also wanted to give her perhaps one last hug and thank her for all that she'd done for me.

At first, I didn't recognize her. She looks great! But she doesn't look like the Mom I knew. That was difficult. And of course, she didn't know who I was. I was prepared for that. If she'd have asked me to leave, I would have. But I could see in her eyes that I was like a memory just out of reach, a slightly fuzzy photo.

Interestingly, it wasn't until I showed her a picture of he and I at the Junior Prom that I saw the "inner light" kick on. I wasn't sure it was the right thing to do, but something told me to get out my iPad and do it. She traced his face on the picture, which enlarged it. She wasn't the least bit spooked by the sudden transition. She couldn't take her eyes off his soft brown eyes. I still don't think she had me placed totally, but her love for that son was palpable, and I sensed that she knew (whoever I was) that I was a friend, and had cared for him, her and the rest of her family.

She spoke of him in the present tense, and I did nothing to dissuade her of that. For me, it was a comfort to speak of him as if he were still alive, odd as that seems. I know that he is in a better place, and I'm so happy about that because he suffered greatly. But, to sit with her once again as I had in my 20s and talk about this man …. It soothed my soul, though it makes me misty thinking about it now. I was so happy that she did not come into the present. I love her dearly, she stood with me when I needed her, and I didn't want to rob her of one minute of her life to grief if I didn't have to. Thankfully, the visit was more than I could have hoped for and if it is the last time we meet here, I can live with that.

Lora is an amazing woman. She is either a like you or not kind of person. I have friends that dislike her, others that would do anything for her. It's just how she rolls. Even yesterday she was pissed off that they had cut her hair so short. You need to understand that this is a person who always took great pride in her looks and took very good care of herself. She wore the reddest lipstick EVER. I couldn't have carried it off, but she was flawless. Her life was not a bed of roses, for a lot of reasons. Not unlike all of us. But she always moved forward. I think that pissed people off. She didn't suffer fools lightly.

I'm having difficult describing the feeling of being there with her, because I want to cry. And I don't know why. It was a good visit. Yes, she has slipped away mentally for the most part, and knowing her, I'm sure that was the most devastating diagnosis she could ever have gotten. That hurt when I was there, knowing that. But yet, sitting on that couch with her, in front of a fire, looking at pictures, I knew that somewhere in her, she knew I was there. And when I left, she wanted my address to write to me. She didn't want to lose touch.

I cannot possibly explain to her that she and I are bound together with a thread that will never break. We will never lose touch. I pray that God is good to her. She has carried so many on her shoulders, and lived such pain. Such a remarkable mother to one and second mother to another. I am so very lucky.

Next?

The past few days have been, for me, days of extremes. Extreme feelings, extreme speech, extreme actions. I'm not a shy, retiring type of person as a rule, but neither am I one, at least at this age, to pitch a bitch. It has been an amazing week.

I spent Monday in my past and present. I went home to renew my spirit. I am not going to lie - I visited the resting places of people I love and miss, and I had conversations with them as well. It was a wonderful day of peace, reflection, and thanks.

Monday was also a watershed day in my relationship with my husband. I'm not all about (at least at this time) taking my dirty marital laundry public, but I will say that, for the first time in our relationship, I refused to be disrespected any more. That may seem a simple thing to most of you. For me, not so much. I have searched my soul for years for the answer.

And the answer came to me so calmly and quietly in a conversation with dear friends at work the other day - the clown has to hide the pain by distracting with a red nose and top hat.

The very quick glib answer here is that I have a very low self-image/respect, blah blah blah. All of that is true. But something is changing. And it's amazing. I have had the very great fortune of meeting a woman who has certain gifts that I will not have. This isn't some mumbo jumbo, it's very much God and spiritually based. And she has opened doors for me. Doors that I had refused to open. Doors that are freeing me.

Through my spiritual work with her, I am learning to see my worth. It seems such a simple action, doesn't it? But I wish you all could be in my space right now. It's like a panoramic vision of life. It's seeing the "little" things that come to us in spirituality. Put simply, it's learning to discern that some who "love" you may not just NOT love you, but they may want to deceive you, harm you, control you, possess you, bully you, and live through you because they have no soul, or at best an empty one.

And who is the best victim for this predator? He or she who feels guilt for past deeds, has a bad self-image, doesn't recognize the gifts they are blessed with. I mean, you can't very well put up a fight if you don't think you're worth it.

I remember, with great shame, one of the worst moments of my life. I spanked my daughter once when she was little, because she did something that scared me. And I was angry and disappointed with myself for a long time.

Several years ago, when I still had the pleasure of her living here with us, she came out of the bathroom after a shower, and I said "don't go downstairs. Dave is in a really bad mood." What that meant was the Dave was looking for a victim, someone to take out his frustrations on verbally.

My beautiful young adult daughter looked at me and said "why do you let him do this to you?" .. and I slapped her and called her ungrateful. I wanted to die. Right there and then.

Why? Because she was right. And I had failed her and my son. All I wanted was a family and security for them. I so believed this was the answer. As it turns out now, even that which I sought is based on lies. Calling her ungrateful was ... how do I want to say this ... projection much?

I have tried to leave this relationship a couple of times, and felt guilty. Felt responsible for someone else's happiness at the expense of my own. As my dear Lisa said, the life has been sucked out of me. I knew it. Everyone knew it.

And I asked myself: what if my beautiful daughter was living the way I was. I was sick to my stomach.

So, on Monday when I returned from my renewing trip home, the line was crossed for the last time. I stood up for myself for the first time. And I called him on his behavior. And I told him he would never disrespect me again.

These are words I've said in my brain a hundred times. This time they came out. And they stuck. Boy did they stuck. Not with him. With me. Now I feel some strength coming back. My prayers are honest and forthright.

I don't know how this will all resolve. But I will tell you that I am not the same person I was three days ago. And there will never ever be enough time in this lifetime to thank those who have lifted me. And God willing, I will be able to prove to my children that I can set an example of being successful and happy and safe.

Stepping out of the Comfort Zone

LOL .. I'm so bad. I love how I just take that deep swan dive into the unknown! Sometimes I wonder if I really did hurt myself when I fell out of the attic when I was three. True story. Remember those pull down attic steps? Those were what we had. Dad and I were up in the attic checking the mouse traps, in our matching trendy sweatshirts I might add, Mom called from the foot of the stairs - I leaned over and BAM. Quickest trip EVER between two floors in a house! Anyhoo, I fell on my head. Boink. Just like in the comics. Mom was several (make that MANY) months pregnant with that which was not chocolate, and she couldn't even bend over to see if I was okay. LOL! I am not even sure Dad climbed or flew down the stairs. I was okay. I'm a tough cookie. Of course, I may have a massive hematoma in my brain that is a ticking time bomb, but hey .. that would explain the migraines. See? There is always an upside.

My marriage is in deep trouble. I'm not sure where it will end up. I am totally out of my comfort zone. I am not used to protecting myself. I do that for others, but not myself. And don't be like .. what a baby. The truth is that very few of us look out for ourselves. We accept things and we work within frameworks, even if those don't work out for us totally. It takes a lot of nuts to start over. I KNOW I can do it if I have to, but I just am not 100% on the details right now. What I DO know, is that no decisions will be made in haste (as opposed to the past), and that there will be (hopefully) a mutual understanding of why this is necessary.

In thinking about potential changes, I have gotten past my material issues - obviously my financial situation is going to change. I think that was a tough one, it's a hard stretch. But, the "possessions" haven't made us happy, so what's the point of holding onto that as a reason for anything. I'm not sure why that was such a big hurdle for me, but I think it's because this was

really the first permanent "home" I'd created for my kids. But ..
they are off on their own (quite successfully, I might add) and
while they have established memories in this house, some are not
so great. So .. that may end up being a wash. Still feel guilty for
screwing it up.

I talked to both of them today and both are supportive. So
weird to feel like you need to get your kids' permission. No,
permission isn't the right word. Approval. Understanding.
Unfortunately the dysfunctionality of the situation extends a bit
into my relationship with them. I'll be grateful when the drama is
over. So grateful.

So my comfort zone seems to be shrinking now. It's okay.
Change is scary and change is critical. I'm not the first person to
be in this position, nor is this the first time I've been in this
situation. But it feels very strange and very different and not a
little scary. I have to consciously guard against being weak. What
a shitty place to be in my life. Seriously.

Meh. When things get difficult, I'll sing "Let it Go" really
really loud.

God help anyone within 15 miles of ground zero.

Buds

There are buds on the trees outside my windows! Spring is upon us, FINALLY! My favorite time of the year. Renewal, rebirth ... all positives. And that is where I choose to be. Positive. I haven't always faced forks in the road with optimism, or even courage, but this time, I'm drawing on both.

My friend Scott told me a story of woman who started her own business. It grew exponentially. She sold it. The franchise became very ordinary. Why? Because her uniqueness was missing. They offered the same product, but they lost her essence. The franchise lives on, and while quality has suffered, profits have not. She opened a new place, with the old product. Not because she needed the money, but because she believed in herself and what she brought to the table in terms of her "ownness".

Change is not only inevitable in all of our lives but necessary. But when changes come, as Scott pointed out, it's important that you retain the essence of who and what you are. Otherwise, it's just a knock off. Not genuine, not original. No one's life is immune to change and upheaval. And what could cause me to want change might seem ridiculous to you, and vice versa. But it doesn't matter. What matters is you, and that you retain the specialness that is you.

I think too often we let things blind our vision with superficiality. We live in the immediate, we react to the little things because the big things seem insurmountable. But to quote Frank Underwood, the best way to devour a whale is one bite at a time. That's where I am, with spring, renewal, rebirth ... taking the insecurities and anxieties and negatives and devouring them one bite at a time. And with each bite, I am going to focus on reinforcing me. Not as someone's wife, mother, employee, friend, aunt .. whatever. As me. Scott is right. No matter what you do, or where you go, you gotta take "me" with you. And damn if I know why "me" gets such a low priority. Rebirth, redemption, renewal. Faith.

Bricks in the Wall

Today has been a day of re-do's for me. First, I left home and made it just about to work before realizing that I'd left my work laptop in the dining room. So, back I go. Then I write a blog post, only to have it not save. On top of that, for some reason, IT cannot figure out why I am not able to access my boss's calendar correctly and they keep taking control of my desktop. Lemme tell you. That's not always a good thing.

So here I am. A re-do. Bear with me. For some reason, I seem to do my deepest thinking on the way into the office. Since I had two shots at deep thinking while driving this morning, I had a brief moment of clarity. I'll share.

Tomorrow I have an appointment with the foot doctor. I have an ongoing problem in my right foot. It hurts and it swells up on the top of the foot, where one would lace up shoes. For months I thought it was my running shoes being wrong – so I have a new pair, and find that the pain/swelling remain. This foot has been through hell. It has supported my ginormous bulk for 59 years, and I have broken the ankle and on another occasion, an entire bone. That's resulted in a bunion, pushing the big toe to the right, foot all out of alignment. Now. Please don't take this as complaining – I'm really not. If they told me it's aging and I gotta live with it, I can do that.

But, I've set a lot of personal goals for 2014 that involve using my feet. That would include some 5ks, and the big 10k across the Bay Bridge in November. Obviously my foot is involved in these endeavors. So tomorrow I see the foot doctor. Best case scenario – orthotics that will take pressure off the muscles and tendons. Worst case? Stress fracture and/or torn tendon. That will require a cast. I would have my choice of soft (removable) cast or hard cast. I will choose the latter BECAUSE otherwise, I will remove the soft cast when the immediate attention-drawing drama of it is over, and ruin the effort to fix the problem. I know me pretty well.

So, I'm pondering this on the way into work (the second time), and I was thinking about how the feet support the body – the muscles, bones, tendons, etc. – and how difficult that must be. And I thought that, while I exercise pretty regularly, I don't do anything (other than buy new shoes) to help my legs and feet accommodate those needs. No stretching, no warm up, no nothing. Just turn on the treadmill or the yoga video and have at it. I think it's a miracle that I can still walk actually.

Then my thought of the day popped into my head. What about our emotional muscles? I don't think we exercise them enough. Or perhaps overdo, without warm up. Think about it. If you cry out loud, you're a wuss. Even though your heart may be breaking or you are in physical pain. If you are depressed, you are a drag to be around and everyone is tired of the moping. After all, you are bumming them out and who wants that? Or, if you laugh hysterically like a hyena, you should probably be medicated in an institution. I tend to do ALL of these things. I'm probably lucky I have any friends and am not in white jacket somewhere.

But, on the whole, don't you think we're going about it wrong? Hiding our emotions so as not to make others uncomfortable. Ignoring other's obvious pain or discomfort because it's uncomfortable for us to express emotion toward them? Physical connection is a whole OTHER animal. No one hugs anymore. But that's a topic for another day.

I have a piece of advice, not just from the cheap seat, but from someone who is viewed as "different" by many. Fuck it. If you feel it, own it. If not, you WILL end up with weak emotional muscles. And you will push them too hard. And when that fall comes, it will hurt – you will cry. So, it's inevitable. Be easy with yourself. Love yourself and feel for yourself. Truth is, you may be the only person in the universe that really does feel for you. Don't drown in it, use those muscles to hold you up. But stop weakening yourself by ignoring you.

Happy Adoption Day!

Two huge events in my life transpired on March 1. This is the first of them. I wish I knew what to call this. Happy Adoption Day? Happy Homecoming Day? Not really sure, but just really glad it happened. Over the years I've accumulated information, spoken to biological parents, taken shit from extended "family" members for not being a real Haacke, busted my neighbor Beth in the mouth and off a fence railing for making fun of my being adopted … it's all part of the most fortuitous thing to ever happen to me.

I was born on November 7, 1954 at Union Memorial Hospital in Baltimore, Maryland. My original name on my birth certificate was Johanna Lynn. Yes, there was a last name and yes, there were parent names on the birth certificate. I am respecting their privacy by not disclosing their names, but I will not protect their character. If you are expecting me to sing their praises, you're in for a shock.

Mom and Dad never misled me in any way about my adoption. Ever. I was told from the time I was old enough to understand. They didn't believe they could conceive, so they adopted me from an Episcopalian adoption agency in Baltimore. My biological mother's family was German, as was my Dad's. Apparently that was pretty much it on the screening process. Information was available to them to some degree about the biological parents, but it is ridiculously inadequate. "Good health". Okay.

My biological parents are alive, she resides in Maryland, he resides in Florida. They worked together – he was a graduate of Western Maryland working for an oil company in Baltimore. She was a secretary. I've spoken to them both. She says she was just "another notch on his belt". He said he didn't know who she was. She said he never knew about me. He finally admitted to dating her a couple of times. I think we all see this handwriting on the wall.

She was packed off to the Florence Crittendon home where I am sure she drilled her well manicured fingernails on the table between cigarettes just waiting for this mistake to be behind her. She never told him she was pregnant. Clearly she knew better than anyone that he could care less. And so it happened that I was born. She never saw me, and I was taken away immediately and packed off to … whomever.

When I contacted "him" (understand it was all done very discreetly), his first comment to me was "the peeping tom conviction was unfair". Great. A sex offender, albeit pillar of the community. She never told her (now deceased) husband anything about any of this. How do you live that lie? She has two sons and a daughter, and he has two daughters and a son. So, I am the oldest of seven children to whom I am biologically related but do not know. I have seen pictures of my siblings on her side on Facebook. I've never approached them and won't.

I was in a foster home from my birth until March 1, 1955 when my parents came to pick me up and bring me home to Chestertown. I have no memory of any of this. Probably just as well. My parents were very excited (I'm told) and our little family was born. Four years later, my sister Terri would be born naturally, as would Debbi two years after that. My parents always credited me with their newfound ability to have their own children. I was so pleased with my sister's birth that I tried to suffocate her. I think that speaks for how pampered I was for four years. And the insecurities of an adopted child. After all, you were picked out, can't you be taken back?

It's difficult to describe what it's like to be adopted, and no one person's story is the same as another. For me, the best description of how I felt was of being an island connected to the mainland by a bridge. I never doubted that I was loved by my

98

parents, ever. But from the beginning, I knew I was "different". I was labeled adopted and my sisters were not. It made a difference. Never in the love from my parents, just in my mind.

Not all of my father's family was understanding or politically correct. I was frequently referred to (in front of me) as "Dave's adopted daughter". I kinda felt for Mom, I mean it's not like she wasn't part of the equation as well, but then again, my Mom never really passed muster with Dad's family either. I always hurt for her on that actually, but she was a steel magnolia. And if their rudeness provoked her, she never let on – to her children.

I'd seen my Dad angry, but never so angry as when someone referred to me as the adopted one. It infuriated him, embarrassed and hurt me, and it was something that he could not control. Something that hurt his child. And make no mistake. For my Dad, I was his child. End of story. My mom always loved me as her child, but she was more open to the idea that I had other biological connections. Not Dad.

I don't even know when my sisters found out. My youngest sister found my adoption papers when she was cleaning out the attic. She was in her teens, I believe. It just wasn't something that we sat around and discussed.

Long and short of it, I was blessed. Were there adjustment issues to deal with? Of course. Were there moments when I wanted to believe some wealthy movie star was my "real" mother? Yeah. Did I wonder about it all? Of course. Did I throw it back in their faces when I got pissed off? Yeah, once or twice. But over all, it was good. Very good. And I loved them very much. So March 1 is a day of celebration for me. Of happiness and gratitude.

My Dad

And today is the birthday of the one who has shaped me the most. I'm not saying this to take anything away from anyone, not my Mom, not my kids, not the men who I have loved and who loved me, nor the many many friends who have had my back – each and every person who crosses your path helps to shape you. To my way of thinking, moral fiber, belief systems, idea of right and wrong – these are the foundation of one's life. These are the building blocks we expand on – embracing some, discarding some, modifying some. And while my mother, sisters, family and friends all had huge impacts on the refinement of these building blocks, it was my father who, by example, set the standards for my life. So

HAPPY BIRTHDAY DAD!!!!!!

There are so many complex dynamics in a father/daughter relationship. One lesson I learned from Dad is that he and I would never agree on everything, and in fact, virtually nothing that was of superficial value. But on the basics we would agree, though sometimes grudgingly. Allow me some looks back now …

For perhaps the last time in our lives as a family, my sisters allowed me to deliver a eulogy to Dad at his memorial service. I am estranged from my sisters, I believe it to be a mutual choice but I also believe that my father would have considered it the biggest failure in his life. That makes me sad because I feel as though I have failed him. But you cannot force square pegs into round holes, no matter how much you want to do so. My sisters and I are very different, and while Mom and Dad lived, they bound us together. Now that both are gone, the glue came apart. I love them both and wish them well, and I hope my Dad doesn't feel it is a failure, because regardless of whether we girls are close are not, or understand each other, or even like each other, we are all strong women with successful lives of our own. I will always wish them well.

Anyway, here is a snippet from that eulogy:

When I first started getting my thoughts together about speaking today, I wondered how I'd ever be able to do my father justice. I had the great good fortune yesterday to listen as Rev. Henry Thompson, Past Worthy Grand Master Ron Belanger, and Dad's dear friend, Morley Frech eulogized my father as both a man and a Mason. It was such a touching and fitting tribute to Dad, and I found myself wondering what more I could add. As if to underscore that, a line from a popular song from the 60s kept running through my mind .. "how do you thank someone who has taken you from crayons to perfume". Such a small sentence, but such an enormous sentiment. Such a daunting task.

And so it was. How do you thank that person? I don't think you can. Ever. Enough. My relationship with my father was not all my Little Ponys. In fact, for a very long time, there was a very black period that was filled with disrespect, disgust, anger, distance, emotional angst, and I truly was not sure I ever wanted to fix it. I did. And he did. But it took a very long time, and more years than I want to admit. But we finally put down the swords and shields and talked and listened. I also had children myself by then and I could put myself in his shoes finally. I understood where he was coming from, but even understanding cannot always mend hearts broken by ugly words. That came with time. And maturity, on both of our parts.

From my eulogy:

Dad garnered many titles during his life, but I know that the ones most important to him were son, brother, husband, father, grandfather, and friend. That was the true essence of my father. His compassion for others. His courage and strength in the face of overwhelming odds. His fierce loyalty and devotion to those he loved. His absolute and unwavering love for his family. His spiritual devotion to God and his belief in the inherent goodness in everyone. And while he could seem intractable at times, my father never expected less of anyone than he expected of himself. And that is perhaps the most enduring legacy that he leaves for us – the standard by which we have been taught to live our lives. Can there be any greater gift that a parent can give?

I don't believe there is any greater gift. Nor do I believe I could have learned that from anyone else. And if I am loved, respected, cared about and for, it is because of what I learned from Dad about compassion and loyalty. As to the "intractable" comment. Well. Yes. LOL! No one who knew my father would dispute that.

I'm going to close this post with this quote from the eulogy. Those who know me are aware that I love to talk, but not unlike anyone else, sometimes I keep my deepest close to me unless it needs to be dusted off and offered if needed to help someone else. These words are perhaps the deepest I have, cannot be recreated by me in any way, and stand the test of time. I love you Dad! Happy Birthday! You are loved and missed more than you know! Or maybe you DO know!

I have been blessed more than most, I think. I was <u>fortunate to be chosen</u> by this most remarkable man to be his daughter. To be loved and cherished and guided by such strong and gentle hands. There aren't words to express how grateful I am now, and have always been, that our roads converged. I thank God that He believed in me enough to give me such a gift. My love for my father is and will always be all encompassing, and my gratitude boundless.

In the late 80s, I worked for a wonderful attorney in Rockville, Camilla O. McRory. Camilla was one of the first attorneys to develop an elder law practice. When I first came aboard, she was doing some general family law in addition to developing this new type of practice. Camilla was one of the most compassionate people I'd ever known, understood before it was hip that we need to take care of our seniors. Not that it's important, but she and I are the same age, so she would have been in her early 30s when she began protecting elder rights. Pretty damn impressive. I was with her for six years. During that time I went from usingan IBM Selectric and carbon paper to an IBM computer with a floppy drive. And THAT required lots of effort on my part to move her forward!

One of the best examples of her foresight into the elder law practice was her hiring of a staff social worker to liaison with the clients. Many of our folks were in nursing homes and retirement communities, and the majority of their family was geographically distant, and some were emotionally distant. Enter Laurie Weiss Braunstein, social worker and huge heart extraordinare. So our little group was formed and moved forward.

In one of her last family law cases, Camilla took on a *pro bono* representation of a teen aged young lady who was in her final trimester of pregnancy. She wanted to give her baby up for adoption. Laurie was dispatched to meet with this young lady, and we moved forward toward her due date.

In the event you're not familiar with Rockville, I don't know if there are more attorneys in Rockville per square foot than in DC, but I would not be surprised. The law firm assigned to represent the adopting parents was located in the office next to ours. That made getting papers signed much more expeditious … faxes were just coming into vogue.

Long and short, our client goes into labor and has the baby. Laurie attends to our client, the papers are signed, and the baby is given to its adopting parents, who were childless. Everyone goes their separate ways to pick up the pieces of their lives.

However, in Maryland, there is a period of time during which the biological parents can …. well … change their minds. Kind of a like a right of rescission. And yeah. That's what happened. Our young client, at the urging of her mother, decided to revoke the adoption. I think it's important to be very clear here that her decision seemed based more on the wants of her mother than her own. She was still in high school. The adopting parents were childless professionals. So, at the end of a week together, they were asked to surrender their child.

This young woman's decision turned out to be a watershed event in my own life. Who knew? If you followed the blog, you know that I am adopted. So, I struggled from the beginning with our handling this case. But, after the baby boy was born, I figured that all's well that ends well. I was so very wrong.

It was decided that the adopting parents would bring the baby boy back to their attorney's office (next door to ours), and we would get the baby, and once they had left the building, would call the mother and have her come pick the baby up. The phone rang late in the afternoon, and Camilla told me that the baby was ready to be picked up. Laurie was also in the office, but Camilla asked me to go and do this. Yes, she knew I was adopted, and yes, it seems an odd thing to do. I begged her to let Laurie do it, but .. no, I was sent to do it.

I went next door and was taken into a conference room where the parents, their attorney and staff, and the baby waited.

For me. To take out of their arms and give to someone else. Not the court, not the baby's grandmother, not any of the attorneys involved … me. An adopted child. I close my eyes now and I can see, hear, and smell that room. The baby powder, the tears of each person in the room (including myself), and a baby's little fist in the air. I was handed the baby, the diaper bag and other things, and I turned around and walked out of the room. I have to say that if the parents had said my name, I might have turned around, given them back the baby and quit my job. But, they didn't, and I took the baby next door, turned him over to Laurie for safekeeping, and tried to wrap my sanity around what had just happened.

I refused to stay in the office for the "swap". Seeing that baby handed off again would have been more than my psyche could have stood. I was furious with the system (one of many times). To me, it should always be about the child. And I don't mean just talk the talk, walk the walk. Yet, I am not willing to tread heavily on that young mother's neck. I am a mother. And an adopted child. The couple had resources that the young woman did not have, and probably (and I say probably because I cannot possibly know anything more than the situation as it existed at that time) could have given that little boy more options than he might have received. But, he would have grown up knowing he was different and might never have known his biological mother. Not unloved, different. Pluses, minuses – isn't that life?

And I, who at 30+ years older than he, wanted to take him home with me, and love him. And tell him he wasn't different, he was <u>wanted</u>. And I wished with everything I had that he was as lucky in his life as I had been. I'm not sure I realized just how lucky until that day.

I packed up my one year old daughter, and we made the trek to the Eastern Shore. And I hugged my parents. Like I'd never hugged them before.

Heart Sugar

Today is Ash Wednesday. The beginning of Lent. The beginning of the celebration of Easter. It's traditional to "give up" something for Lent for the purpose of "the preparation of the believer through prayer, penance, repentance of sins, almsgiving, atonement, and self-denial." [courtesy of Wiki] ... This all of course to be done in preparation for the crucifixion and resurrection of Christ on Easter Sunday. Since I am Christian, I am prepared to give something up for Lent. Yesterday I wondered if I could possibly choose between chocolate or ice cream (there is some SERIOUS self-denial there .. trust me) ...

Today, I choose to give up anger. It may take me a full six weeks to get a handle on this, but it's my choice. I don't mean anger in a generic sense, but a specific anger that I carry inside and that crushes me when I let it out of its box. It's an anger directed at certain people for perceived slights and injustices. It's an immature, irrational anger because it comes from a place deep inside of me, a place called insecurity and ego.

If you were my friend and I told you the facts of this situation, you would no doubt empathize with me and love me, which really would gratify my inner child. Or you might tell me to grow up and let it go. Or you might tell me to STFU. And I would love you for whatever you said, but it wouldn't change me inside.

I would still hurt, hold a grudge, be angry and get a headache over it. What I choose to do for Lent is to let it go, with all of the attendant issues. If severing needs to be done, I will do it. I am the only one who is hurt by my anger and resentment. And Christ would have forgiven years ago, I'm still nursing the grudge.

So, my wish for all this Lent and Easter season is peace. Nothing is worth more than that. And the only place you will find that is in you. God Bless.

[and NO smartasses, I am not talking about my husband. LOL!]

[at least .. not this time]

[Rock on]

Little Piece of Your Heart

I am trying to process a powerful piece of reporting that I read tonight. It's the first public comment ever by Peter Lanza, the father of the Newtown shooter, Adam Lanza. Adam killed twenty children. He also killed adults, including himself and his mother. But he killed children. Elementary school children.

There is such weight behind those words. Such unspeakable horror. The worst nightmare of any parent or teacher. Even with the uptick in school shootings, I think there is an element of "it won't happen to me". I get that because, as a human being and parent, the fear that sending your baby out into the world generates is incomprehensible. If you allow yourself to go there, you'll go insane. So, when the Adam Lanzas of the world throw themselves into the path of our consciousness, we immediately band together to find the enemy. Even if that enemy is illness.

But what if you are the parent of one of these diseased, imperfect miscreants? Do we blame you? Do we feel sorry for you?

Peter Lanza wishes his son had never been born. Think about that. Erase a sibling or friend or even just an acquaintance from your life. Here is a parent wishing their child had not been born. Peter Lanza recognized that things were wrong. He knew that his son was not right. He knew that his ex-wife was sheltering a child who couldn't cope with our reality. He did the best he could. And now he wishes his child had never been born.

If you read the article, it traces Adam's life, and it's clear to anyone reading it that this kid was on a short train to nowhere. His mother, out of love and protection for a child with autism, over compensated for him – which cost her a marriage, and ultimately her life. His father, with whom Adam was at one time close, watched both his ex-wife and son deteriorate. Nancy Lanza became a virtual puppet of Adam Lanza. And when Adam Lanza shot his mother, he did so four times – his father believes it symbolic - that was one shot for each member of their family.

Peter Lanza doesn't place blame, he just sees his son as a monster. Some of us might say that's not "fair", that the child needed help that he didn't get [not the case] or that his mother was over protective, resulting in his actions [maybe the case]. Doesn't matter. It just rips your heart to shreds to think of a parent who wishes their child hadn't been born. But what is his alternative?

To see the smiling pictures of the 20 elementary school children dead by his son's hand? How do you live with that? Peter Lanza has tried to sort it out. And the best he's been able to come up with is that he wishes his son had not been born. I can't imagine the torment behind that thought.

In other news, George Zimmerman signed autographs at a gun show today.

This isn't about gun control, it's about unanswerable questions. Short of killing him themselves, what could the Lanza parents do? They consulted with doctors, they did what they were told. He was just defective. There was no place to return him and get a newer model. They tried to accommodate his growing psychological needs, but they outgrew everyone, and ultimately consumed them.

Could Adam Lanza have been been made whole and well? Doubtful. Should he have had access to guns? Probably not. Was Nancy Lanza surprised when he killed her? As a parent, I say probably not. But which of us would ever be able to accept that in our child? Wouldn't any of us have done what they did? Try to make it right? Try to help a child that was so dangerously damaged, it was beyond their comprehension?

I don't know how Peter Lanza lives with this. He said he refuses to think of the child Adam once was, when there weren't as many problems. Because the pain is too severe. I get that.

And George Zimmerman is giving autographs.

Has nothing to do with gun control or any legislation. Has everything to do with preserving the rights of everyone at the cost of all. I wish I knew the answer. Just a tragedy of enormous proportions across the board. None more so than to the surviving Lanzas who must answer questions they don't know the answers to.

Thank you

Once upon a time, there was a young, confused teenager. As is the teenager way, she didn't know she was confused. Into her life came a strong young man. One who enjoyed music and fun. One who could make her laugh, and who made her feel valued. They "loved" the way teenagers do ... And made a very common teenage mistake. In fact, the girl herself was a product of just the same mistake.

Because of the family's "prominence", this type of mistake must be hidden behind prestigious walls, false names, etc. But more damning to the young girl was the venomous condemnation of the two who raised her and who now sought to relocate her "for her own sake".

The young man was banished from the home, warned never to grace it's gates again. Since the young man was her only confidant, his absence broke her heart and made life even more desolate. Then, miraculously, one evening, at the gates, there stood the young man. He asked to see The Lord of the Manor. Alone.

Sometime later, The Lord of the Manor appeared and revoked the restrictions placed on the young people and they went on through the resolution of their issue with each other's support.

The courage that this young man showed by challenging The Lord of the Manor is amazing, but even more than that, to have lifted a damned daughter from a home of recrimination and hurt, and try to show her that she was still alive and had a life to live that wasn't over? Well, that took more compassion and strength then I ever felt deserving of.

I know your days are difficult, and the old details aren't important anymore. Just know that you changed me from being bitter and self-consumed to someone who danced to her own song.

Love you so very much my dear friend. I think of you every day. God speed.

- Do men get stupid after they get married, or do women get stupid to get married?

- Why is there a random shopping cart on a street 10 miles from the nearest store?

- Time does not heal all wounds. God does, if it's in the plan. Otherwise, deal with it.

- Why don't people chew with their mouths closed?

- Is there anyone who hasn't peed in the shower?

- Anyone else want to put a bullet hole through their TV at Christmas with respect to the ASPCA?

- Hit "send" without noticing the "cc"? Oooops.

- Ever wondered if you said something out loud or just thought it?

- If you're female: Ever passed gas in public? If you're male: Ever NOT passed gas in public?

- Ever ass ended a police car? C'mon. There has to be someone other than me.

- Don't you hate it when you get caught picking your nose? It seemed like a safe time …

- Don't you love seeing someone scared out of their minds? The only thing that tops this for entertainment value is seeing someone fall down!

- Water ever broken when you weren't pregnant?

-    How many times have you looked at someone and said "Seriously?" because they're stupid?

-    Ever had to straight face someone at karaoke and say they were good when you wish you were deaf and mute? And maybe even blind?

-    Ever face palmed when your friend/date/significant other said something so stupid in public that only they believed?

-    Wondered who the hell comes up with clothes at "Fashion Week" in Milan? An alien?

-    Ever had your small child mangle a word in public just to the point of sounding like a small bigot?

Life goes on.

Terms of Endearment

Dear Kathi,

Sometimes even I am astonished by the things you do. Most of the time I know what you're going to do, but there are times you surprise me – like today.

You were going to put on your big girl panties and get over your anger, deal with your frustration, accept that sometimes it's not you that causes issues, issues happen to you because of someone else. Really, you were going to let go and let God.

You certainly screwed this up.

Yep, right out of the box. Lent .. is it even a week old yet? When will you learn that knee jerk reactions only cause pain, usually yours? When will you learn that even when you are right, you don't have to say so, and you don't have to crucify others to feel good about yourself.

Now, to be fair to you, you have gone through a lot with respect to this issue. These people were not good to, or for, you. You feel like you owe them something because they're "family". They were not people you would select for friends or who you thought trustworthy. But they are people. And they are people you shared part of your life with. That alone earns them the right not to have been battered like you did today. So you owe them an apology.

Ummmm

This assumes they give a shit. This assumes they don't feel the same way. This assumes it upset them at all, and it really assumes they care what you think.

Do they?

No.

And that's what you can't get past. That you meant that little. But you will get past it. Because for once, you did the right thing, albeit in the wrong way.

Give yourself a wedgie with those big girl panties, cry it out, and then go for a run. This is going to bother you for a long time. But it's your problem, not theirs. And your problems, you can control.

Love,

Kathi xoxo

Toxic

I had the best dream last night. I think we're foolish if we don't accept the validity of our dreams (if we can remember them). I dreamt that I was in a tornado and rather than being buffeted by the wind, a beautiful blue sky opened in the midst of it and engulfed me. There was more to the dream but it was personal to me and I don't need to share it. The point is that yesterday I ended two lifelong relationships that were tumultuous and toxic for me, but yet I felt bound by convention to honor the relationships.

I have come to realize that no one HAS to love you – not a parent, child, sibling, friend. Love is earned, it is not a title that you are born with. Nor do you have to love anyone. I am hearing more and more stories from peers who either struggle or have struggled with accepting that the love bonds we expect to feel, or "should" feel, are sometimes less satisfying than we want them to be. I am not talking "relationship" love, I speaking of the unconditional love we expect from parents, siblings, children. Convention dictates that those are inviolate love relationships. Yet I find that many of us AARPers feel empty when it comes to our parents or siblings. And I think that we feel like the disconnect is entirely our fault for the most part.

It is not. I have learned that parents have feet of clay (not gold), that they are human and imperfect, and do make mistakes. I have learned that siblings are not necessarily people you like or respect. I have learned that it is really okay to be aghast over Great Aunt Mildred's selfishness or see realistically that Uncle Bernie is a creeper. All of these feelings come under the subtitle "Family". And boy howdy, don't go to that subject if you're not going to show it the full respect it deserves.

Here's what YOU deserve. You deserve to be respected as the unique individual that you are. You don't have to prove anything to anyone, except yourself. If you believe in God, then you know that he has your back. He knows what's going down in your book. All you owe HIM is taking good care of you. And taking good care of you can mean making hard decisions about people in your life. No one said that any of this was going to be easy, but how good do you feel when you say thank you to someone who has been kind to you? Or listened to you? Or reached out to you? When you think about the positives, it is so much easier to absorb the negatives.

Don't embrace toxins you think you "should", fling yourself at the happys that you WANT. You need to start being selfish.

Twerkin

I work with a [mostly] phenomenal group of people. By and large, they are my kids' ages. This has not been a problem for me, though my peers find it somewhat horrifying. I guess it's because I don't feel "old" and I've always been the oldest person.

Two of my husbands have been seven years younger, one two years older, and one seven years older (yes. Count that. 4. Total. Liz Taylor got nothing on me! Except her money. And she's dead.) So, age is not a big deal to me. In fact, working with this group of people has been a joy, and has helped me rediscover many things that I'd left by the wayside on my way to becoming aged like beef jerky.

So, a couple of Fridays ago, one of us put together a "going away" party of sorts for a colleague who was moving to another department. It started with drinks at an Irish pub, and then moved to a karaoke bar. Now, I love karaoke. I truly do. But I couldn't carry a tune if you PAID me large amounts of money. Almost all of my girl crushes have been female rock stars – Grace Slick, Janis Joplin, Pink, Gwen Stefani, Carly Simon, Karen Carpenter – but, regretfully, a crush was the extent of the relationship. I have never had a singing voice. If I did, Miss Fagan scared it out of me in 6th grade when she made me sing The First Noel by myself to prove I was awful. It worked.

Worse, years of smoking made an alto into a bass. But, regardless, nothing brings me more joy than turning up a song REALLY LOUD in the car with the window down and just belting it!!! Mostly Aerosmith, but sometimes Steppenwolf. NEVER Whitney or Celine. Donald has that covered.

Unfortunately then, my vocal range narrows my song selection choices at karaoke. In fact. I can only sing one song, which is "I Touch Myself" by the Divinyls. Who knew? And I don't sing it very well, it's just that SOMEONE has to sing it. It might as well be me. So I do.

And I did that Friday night. Now, we'd all been sucking down moonshine for a couple of hours, even hubby. And there it is. My call! "Up next … Kathi!" … woooooo hooooo from all my drunk friends, high five from my uber talented singing friend Jason. And up I go.

"I love myself, I want you to love me. When I feel down, I want you above me."

All of a sudden … and I shit you not on this … I am being twerked by a bunch of mid-20s redneck guys, slapping my butt with their hats, singing with me .. etc. etc.

HOLY SHIT. Really. HOLY SHIT my husband is on the other side of the bar staring at me. I have crawled up against the wall as close as I can get. There is no room to move. I am captive. And I am laughing and singing my ass off!!! Off key as well!! It was …. fucking AWESOME!

My friends, who have had so much to drink that they aren't even sure what room they're supposed to be in, are torn between worry about my safety with respect to hubby, and chortling wildly at this spectacle. God love my friend Lisa, who sidles up to the bar next to hubby and says drily "I think she's doing a good job of ignoring it". LOL! LOL!

Finally, interminably, it was over. I was laughing so hard, I thought I'd sprung a leak. Hubby held it together until we got in the car, and then was very indignant about my performance. I couldn't even keep a straight face. I think that made the whole situation worse.

We survived it, and it has now become a standard in my comic repertoire.

Twerking. Indeed.

LOL!

Good times, good times. Thank you guys! You know who you are!

I'm a … noun?

Okay, I admit. I was taken aback when I read the statement "stop thinking you are a noun". For those that are confused, a noun is not a verb. A noun is a title. A verb is an action. For instance, "mother" is a noun, "parenting" is a verb. I never got into the whole sentence diagramming, so if that's not quite right, screw off. I'm not even going to adjectives.

I'm a noun. Yes, I am. I am a mother, wife, daughter, administrative assistant, friend, college graduate, car owner, house owner, aunt, etc. The list goes on. So, does this mean that I'm defined by the noun that you see me as, because even if that noun is "asshole", you've classified me as something. Which makes me a noun.

I AM NOT JUST A NOUN. Just want to make that clear to you. Neither are YOU.

Each one of us is multi-layered, flawed, and more than the sum of our parts. Unfortunately, I think we all accept our nouns, and don't focus on our verbs. Why is that?

I laugh, a LOT, about lots of things. Laughing is a verb.

I love, a LOT, many people. Loving is a verb.

I eat, too much sometimes. Eating is a verb.

I write, not always very well. Writing is a verb.

Let's see. So far, I am four verbs. All good verbs, don't you think? Verbs that I couldn't exist without.

I trust people, until they give me a reason not to. Trusting is a verb.

I entertain people, sometimes. Again, a verb.

I piss off people, a lot. Pissing off is not a GREAT verb, but it's an action word, for sure.

My point here is ... embrace your verbs. Yes, you are a noun, but nouns are so ... stodgy. Verbs ..... now THERE are action words. Stop focusing on what you are, and jump out and do. Do the things you WANT to do, that make you happy, regardless of judgment. Make the time to DO for you. Life is too short. Don't live in the past. It's not going to matter. Trust me.

I don't want to be interred anywhere as anything, but if I were to have a grave stone ... I don't want "beloved mother and daughter", I'd want "She made me smile. And ... you're standing on my head".

The Wind Beneath My Wings

The wind beneath my wings. Let's just take Bet Midler *out* of this right now before we all bawl like babies. Truly, that scene in "Beaches" is right up there with Sally Field's soliloquy at the grave of Julia Roberts in "Steel Magnolias". These are 10s on the emotional earthquake meter. "AVOID" "AVOID" ....

But the wind beneath my wings. I always write such dark crap. Always problems, and how to make me a better person, how to become more self-aware, etc. etc. And yes. All of that is valid. It really is. And I have made significant strides. But the truth is that, birds can't soar without wind. No bird gets off the ground without help.

And that's what today is about for me. I've spent the past few hours thinking about my life and just celebrating some of the landmarks along the way that never seem to be talked about. These quiet events, the strength given or taught .. they are the defining moments, I think. And we accept them, thank them, learn from them. But we never really have a moment to tell the story, unless it's in a eulogy. Which, by definition is not a good time to thank someone. So, for the next few days, I'm going to reach back and thank some folks who fly under the wire but who have changed my life in extraordinary ways.

Kim .. we sailed off in our boat to the wonderland that was Radford College, full of expectation and promises. We both carried emotional baggage, yours is yours to share, mine was the stupefying depression that was sinking its teeth into me following my abortion the previous summer. But here it was, we were at COLLEGE, with Deborah Baldwin, 8 hours from home. ON OUR OWN. I didn't handle it well. You did. You had a work ethic and you did what you needed to do. I was too busy running away from myself to accomplish anything. And so, you went on to graduate and I flunked out. To avoid dealing with myself, I married a townie in a super-duper HUGE wedding at the Country Club, and then I went back to Radford with him to married life, while you finished up your sophomore year.

I took a job as an "office manager" in a jewelry store and hated myself more as each day passed. The boy I had married was as immature as I was, so it was really quite the match. I suppose I should have realized this wasn't going to be a good match when he ambushed me in the woods and tried to shoot me before we got engaged. Kids. So silly. WTF?

The long and short of it was that if I thought that this was the solution to my emotional problems, I was really ... really .... really wrong. I married when I was 19, was divorced by 21. I've had colds that lasted longer than that.

But, back to my friend Kim. One thing about Kim, she plays her hand close to chest. Being judgmental is not her thing. Being a friend always was her thing. We grew up together, went to church together, and ran pretty much with the same group in high school (Deborah, Lori, Patty Sue, Patty G., Beth (LOL .. to anyone who knows both Kim's and my issues with that one) and so on). So this was a person whom I trusted, who knew me as well as anyone could have at the time, and I cared about.

At Radford, while on a caving expedition (did you have a crush on the teacher or am I delusional??), she broke her leg, and my Romeo and I put her up at our house for her immediate recovery. Man. That is the first time I really saw physical pain. I felt so badly for her, there seemed so little I could do. And, I have to confess, I am NOT Nancy Nurse. My children will bear that out. But we did what we could to make her comfortable and she stayed for awhile before going back to her dorm.

Time passed and I fell deeper and deeper into the blackness. I was a stranger in a strange land - it was altogether a new and unfamiliar culture. I didn't fit in very well, and my mother-in-law said I had "crazy eyes". This from a woman named Cherokee who had a pet monkey she kept loose in her home. Ahhh memories.

Finally I stopped trying to cope altogether. I just sat on the couch in the living room, listening to Diana Ross and watching test patterns on the TV. If we ate anything, I just put the utensils away after we ate, sometimes I even rinsed them. I was well on my way out. There was no question. I must have been almost 20 at the time.

One day Kim comes over to visit. She unlocks the door and comes in. The stench had to be unbearable. She looked at me in my bathrobe, went upstairs and looked around. Came back downstairs rolled up the sleeves on her shirt, and cleaned, washed, scrubbed, vacuumed, dusted, emptied cat boxes … everything that needed to be done .. until that house was 100% again.

Then she came into the living room and stood in front of me and said "I have done all I can do to help you. Now you have to help yourself. I won't be back until you decide to live again." And she left.

I was mildly annoyed that she dared to speak to me in that way. Real emotion had been tamped down in the depression, but the more time that passed, the more angry I got. Until one day, thank God, I took a shower. I made the choice to live. And unless you have lived in the special hell reserved for depressives, you cannot know what a gift my friend Kim gave me.

Folks, this was ONE day. ONE event. Out of 59 years. This is what makes us who we are. While I was so grateful to her at the time, I am a hundred fold more grateful now. Had it not been for her care, much could have changed in my life. Would I be alive? Have my children? Be able to write? Know and love the friends I have? Who knows?

What I DO know is that I know a woman who set the friendship bar so high that I don't know that I can ever achieve it BUT … and I mean this .. I have and do try because I know what that kind of friendship can mean in someone's life.

So. Thank you Kim Jones McSorley for being the wind beneath my wings.

And I'm sorta sorry I stole your yearbook. Sorta.

The Terminator

Okay, this one comes with a spoiler. It involves drugs. If you want out, you know where the door is.

After writing about my friend Kim yesterday, I got caught up in a nostalgic wave about my first attempt at (1) college and (2) marriage. Unfortunately, my attempts at both of these things result in a combined double digit amount. Obviously not strong suits for me. But today, we're on #2, marriage.

I met Jackie (yes, his real name – good God it was 50 years ago. Who cares now?) when I was attending Radford College. Jackie was a "townie", meaning peeps that lived in Radford and fed off of the all women's college population and naiveté. Actually, that's not quite a true statement (right Kim?) .. the year we went in as freshman, Radford went coed. There were 13 men. A bazillion women. The odds were not real good for the girls. So the options were the gentlemen from Virginia Tech (which Radford was the "girls" side of) or the townies.

The commute to Tech was tiring. Getting back even more so. I lost interest in that right away. I didn't have a car, so it was a matter of finding a ride. Tres difficult. And not worth the selection. In my opinion anyway.

My ridiculously untalented voice major roommate and I had parted ways (she didn't like that I smoked. It wasn't good for her range) and after batching it for awhile, Carol moved in with me. Now Carol was a tiny, Italian, Norfolk Virginia Slims Menthol chainsmoking kinda gal. I loved Carol. We were like Mutt and Jeff. Carol was beautiful. I was not.

Carol hooked up with a dude named Ollie, who was a townie (I am not making this up). And so I was introduced to the Third Street Gang. This would be a group of young people who had grown up together in the same neighborhood (an affluent one at that) and who were like one huge family. And so the fateful meeting with Jackie, husband #1.

One of the local attractions in Radford was Claytor Lake. Most of these kids' parents had spots up there. Really NICE cabins. One night we were all up at Jimbo's parent's place for a soiree. Lots of weed, lots of beer, lots of frivolity. One thing they were into was playing poker. Game went well into the night. One of the guys was naked by the fourth or fifth hand, but I was at the point with this group where it didn't faze me at all and I could even carry on a conversation without looking at the ceiling or my feet. I remember having a little too much of something that night, and being horizontal on the floor. All I could hear was "Top of the World" by the Carpenters. It just kept playing and playing and playing. To this day I have a residual flashback buzz when I hear that song. So it was Karen and Richard Carpenter .... And this weird tapping sound. On the roof of this cabin. In the country. In the dark. Everyone kinda freaked out. Like .. the biggest woodpecker EVER up there.

So we go out, and there you have it .. a giant human naked woodpecker. Yep. On the roof dancing around. It was really kind of awesome. I'm not gonna lie. I mean, I've done some stuff, but … not naked roof dancing.

I had hitched a ride up there with Jackie, and I really wanted to go back to Radford. This was not a do-able walk, and hitching was out of the question. So, I headed out into the darkness to try to find his van. I figured he'd gone to sleep … he and I were not yet an item, so if he got mad at me for waking him up and asking to go home, what's the worst that could happen?

As it turned out, it was being shot at. Yes, yes he did. All I remember was walking toward his van, and the side sliding door opening and someone pushing me from behind to the ground. Then "pinnnnng" over my head. I was like …"HEY. Who pushed me on the ground?" Because of course, I had never ever heard a gun go off in my life except big BOOMS during hunting season. And then I saw the Terminator standing in the light of the van.

I was so pissed. I got up and marched my (then) skinny ass over there and asked for an explanation. Do you know that he just asked me for a date, and I said yes? And this is how I made my way into marriage 1? Oh for god's sake, are you KIDDING me?

Well, not long after that, Carol and Ollie got married in a big ass Catholic wedding in Norfolk. I looked so cute. She had adorable bridesmaids outfits .. they were blue with big wide brimmed hats. Empire waist. I looked so good. Me and the Terminator.

It is worth mentioning that Carol and Ollie remained married until his death some years ago. I am not certain what happened, and I miss Carol to this day. Jackie and I divorced, but only after he chased me back to Chestertown, and I hit him over the head with a fireplace poker in front of my mother.

Good times, good times. So, you ask how I ended up the way I am? LOL!!

Seriously. You cannot make this shit up.

[Editorial note: this blog entry has been *seriously* edited from its original form. Probably to avoid lawsuits]

Parlez vous Francais?

I decided to go back and revisit the Wind Beneath My Wings … you know, the amazing people in your life who change you for the better without meaning, or maybe even knowing. I'm giving tonight's time to Madame Lucette Morris, my 9th grade French teacher. Stop laughing ;)

As most of you know, I was raised in Chestertown, MD … a small town on Maryland's Eastern Shore. Because of my Dad's career, we moved for my 8th grade year to Houston, and then to Summit, New Jersey for 9th grade. Some of you may also know that I was enrolled in an all girls private school, Kent Place School. Please. Just kill me now. All girls? 9th grade. This was not how I pictured my hard partying, weed smoking, making out high school days starting out. For god's sake, we had to wear uniforms. I have no geek in me. I am not the least bit studious. Every single report card in elementary school had check marks next to "needs to practice self-control". An all girls school? OMG. And the rest of my class seemed to have been weaned on blazers and knee socks. I was such an outsider. Plus. I listened to Hair. This didn't bode well.

When we went for my entrance interview, the very upper crust Headmistress (yes, somewhat Dickensian) inquired about the many years of French in my academic record. You see, when I was in fourth grade, Kent County began an experimental language program. We had to all take French. Our book was Ecouter and Parler (Hearingand Speaking). In our book, there was a lesson in French on the front of the page, and translation on the back of the page. Really was not a stretch, considering we were STILL in that book when I departed for 8th grade in Houston. The Headmistress was impressed with the fact that I had taken 5 years of French. I was put in French 9A.

I thought that was cool as shit. I'd never been A anything! So I saunter into my French class and Madame Morris (pronounced Maurice) begins talking. In French. We got our textbooks. They were real ones. No English. My peers were conversing with her like they were native Parisians. I had not a f'ing clue what anyone was saying. I didn't even know when homework was being given out. And no one liked me enough to TELL me that homework had been given out.

Conjugate verbs? WTF is a French verb? I was still on Chapter 4 of Ecouter and Parler, which was roughly equivalent to See Spot Run. Now, they're presenting me with War and Peace. Holy shit.

One of the high points of this school was interim reports. I got one in each of my classes for each marking period. Except maybe Phys Ed. I did get one in Modern Dance. I just couldn't wrap my brain or my leotard around the entire concept. So, Madame Morris is sending my parents these interims telling them I'm failing French. They are like .. Quoi? You're failing French? You've had five years of it.

By this point, I have given up on the whole thing. I'm now being tutored in Algebra (9D), have a C in my best class, English (9C), and World History with Mr. Snow was a disaster. And then, there was Madame Morris, the language labs (big ass headphones repeating over and over "avoir" "j'ai" "tu as" "il a" "elle a" "nous avons" "vous avez" etc. etc.) The verb "avoir" means to have. Really? In English I have, you have, we all have. WTF are all these tenses, masculine, feminine. No wonder the French are flying their freak flag all the time and don't shave under their armpits. They don't have TIME. They are too busy conjugating! [Sorry my French friends, it really is a compliment!]

Long story short, Madame Morris rode me like a very small pony. Up my butt all the time. "You can do better, you are not applying yourself". I'm like .. bitch. If I knew what you were saying, I'd probably cut you.

Finally, FINALLY, in May she spoke to me in English. She told me I was going to fail. And that if I failed the class, I would not be "invited back" to Kent Place School. Seriously? Let's see. You all make an assumption (without testing in any way) about my proficiency, and you're going to fail me out of this school?

I was torn.

So, I locked myself in my bedroom for two weeks and I conjugated until I was producing verbs like Octomom produced kids. I took the final. And I got a B.

And I got invited back to Kent Place School.

And then we moved back to Chestertown, so it didn't matter anyway.

The moral of this thing is that I owe an incredible debt to Madame Morris for stirring something inside of me ... pride. I was not going to be beaten by a bunch of stupid verbs. It was awful. It was humbling, it was mortifying. But I beat it. By myself.

And then it didn't matter because I wasn't going back to Kent Place.

But I was living with myself. And I was AWESOME for a time!

My Baby Girl

Continuing my trend of celebrating those who have (purposefully or otherwise) impacted my life in a meaningful way, today I expose one-half of my heart, my daughter Betsy. There really aren't enough keystrokes to adequately thank her for all that she has done and been for me, not enough pages, for sure. But she and my son, Ian, are 100% of my heart, and have made my life worth living. Were it not for both of them, I don't know that I would still be drawing breath.

Betsy's life has been difficult, probably no more difficult than any of us go through, but as her Mom, of course, I feel the hurts and bumps in the road more keenly. Betsy came into the world via two parents with emotional issues, who were selfish and self-absorbed, and who, after she was born, could not imagine how we had existed before her birth. I need to make one thing exceptionally clear here – Betsy's Dad loved her very much. Very much. Just as he loved me. This is not about him, but he hurt Betsy terribly down the road, and there is little I can do to justify what was done to her, though I have spent decades trying. That is my problem. But she was greatly and gloriously worshipped when she came into this world.

I was just an accessory to their relationship. There was nothing but Daddy and Betsy. He bathed her, I would put her jammies on, and then I was banished. Daddy rocked and read and told stories, and Betsy fell asleep. It was blissful for three years, and then I made a crucial decision and Daddy left our lives for more than a decade. And I had to explain that to a four year old. Actually, I didn't have to and shouldn't have, but it's just one more bad brick in my wall.

Betsy was a petite beautiful baby. Her hair stubbornly refused to grow, and so she had the most precious short curls.

She laughed and laughed, and even as a child showed enormous compassion and love for animals. And, she hated when I put dresses on her.

One day I got a telephone call from her Dad. Betsy was spending the weekend with him and his wife. He said she was talking funny. I thought .. what does that mean. We decided it might just be her doing baby talk to get his attention, and said we would revisit in the morning. In the morning, she was fine. But evening, she was not. She was again having difficulty speaking, and so he brought her home, and I tucked her into bed.

The next morning she seemed fine, again, and we headed to Bowie to have lunch with my parents. I had married Ian's Dad by now, so it was the four adults and Betsy. During lunch, my heart sunk to depths I didn't think were possible. I watched as my four year old appeared to suffer stroke symptoms. She lost control of the left side of her face, and had to use her hand to move her jaw to talk or eat.

Obviously we went directly to Holy Cross. No answers. Maybe a virus? Here have some Amoxicillan. Then, the next day, fine in the morning – by evening, the same symptoms, only much stronger, now it was affecting her coordination and walking. A flurry of pediatric appointments, an MRI appointment. While waiting for the MRI, Betsy got up to walk and hit the floor like an ironing board. She had no control over one side of her body. My beautiful baby girl.

Rick and I immediately took her to Childrens Hospital in D.C. Her Dad and his wife met us there in the emergency room. They brought in the Pediatric Neurologist, Dr. Weinstein. He took the four of us aside and explained that he would be doing a test, injecting a drug and a placebo to test for what he suspected was wrong. He asked us please not to exhibit any reaction to either. The placebo was injected, and no change. The Mestinon was injected, and my child's body straightened back up, her droopy eyes lifted, and she could talk again. Not reacting to that may well have been on my top ten things of hardest to do in my life.

Dr. Weinstein took us aside and said: I have good news and bad news. The good news is I know what is wrong with her, the bad news is she will never be normal again.

What?

What?

Betsy was diagnosed at four years old with Myasthenia Gravis. Remember Jackie O's hubby Aristotle? He had it. It's an old person disease. It's an autoimmune that destroys communication lines between the brain and nerve receptor sites. So, if Betsy's brain said "walk", the legs didn't get the message. The disease progresses during the day – MG patients are at their best in the morning, then as they tire with activity, the disease takes over. The answer to this was medication every four hours to preserve a constant nerve communication level. It was not a fatal disease, per se, but it would re-write her life. A four year old with MG was almost unheard of. Betsy was kept at Childrens and was studied by NIH, Georgetown, and Hopkins. She was remarkably unaffected by the "attention". Her medication was given orally, so she didn't have to deal with shots, although getting blood from her was very stressful because of her fear.

We were told that Betsy would live a normal life, but that she would have difficulty with activity that occurred with stressors: sun, heat, emotion, etc. She probably would not enjoy outside activities. My heart sank as I thought of the roller blading, swimming, biking she would not enjoy again (or so I thought). It was a very difficult time.

Finally we were allowed to come home (I stayed at Childrens with her for two weeks), and I was so happy to put her back in her own little bed. Because her father was spiraling down into the illness that would eventually kill him, he had to remove himself from the situation - it simply required too much emotion from him. So, the decisions for her care were mine alone to make. Rick was a champ, he loved Betsy as if she were his own. So we were just happy to have her home with us.

The first night we were home, Betsy was thrilled to be back in her own bed and settled in her with plushies and stuffed animals. I must have checked on her 100 times. Finally, I went to bed. Rick was watching television, and I picked up a book and pretended to read.

I just stared at the writing. I couldn't comprehend anything. Nothing. It was like the pages were blank. Finally, I pulled the covers up over my head, and for the first time, I cried. I cried like my heart would never heal, I felt pain so great, that I cannot imagine the pain of a parent that loses a child because this pain was enough to kill me. And it might have ... had I not felt a tap on my shoulder. I lifted my head out from under the blanket and there stood Betsy.

"Please don't cry Mommy. I'm going to be okay. I promise".

I have no words.

Except that God has blessed me.

PS: She has been in remission since she was 7. Nothing they predicted happened to her. God is good, believe that.

Thank you my beautiful, intelligent, loving daughter for showing me what is important in life. I have no words for the love I feel for you and your brother.

Self-Doubt

I am going through a crisis of self-doubt. Anyone shocked? I've laid myself bare, yet I call Nancy Grace "exploitive". I'm sorting through the difference, because I know there is one. It's just out of reach for me. What makes me different from Nancy Grace or a plethora of other public figures that have chosen to make their private hells public? What reward is there for this? Obviously I'm not making money off of it. So it's clearly meeting needs for me on some level. I also enjoy entertaining people. And though I may seem off the beam, I really think it's important for people to know that they have made a difference in this world. If you touch and change one person's life for the better, you've made God smile. I'm not trying to earn wings; I'll stand on my own merit. But it brings me to a happy place when I write of good things, and sometimes I feel happy when I write of bad things. None of us are islands or exist in a vacuum. The good and bad things in our lives are shared, just in different ways. We all lose loved ones. We will all die. We will all, at some point, wonder if we made a difference. I look at this journey of mine as a trip down the Amazon. There are always going to be alligators and snakes and breathtaking vistas.

I know that I am not going to write the next great American novel. I can't write fiction – probably because life has proven to be stranger than anything made up in my world. In some worlds, fiction is purely escapism and fantasy. In others, it provides a platform for dealing with crisis. Anne Rice is my favorite author. I liked her vampires, but I loved her witches. You want to know why? In her Mayfair books, she had a character that shared my birthdate. Rowan Mayfair. I became Rowan on some level. I find out later after exchanging a message with her that November 7 is not only the date of Rowan's birthday, but also the birthdates of both Lestat (yes, THAT Lestat) and her husband, Stan Rice. Coincidence? Her husband and the Brat Prince? I think not. I read all the chronicles, but I missed that on Lestat. I've read countless articles on Anne but I missed that on Stan. Why did I absorb it about Rowan? Because I loved her character, and that one personal detail was enough that I could have BEEN her. Rowan became my alter-ego, the same way Scarlett O'Hara had in my teens. That's what fiction does. It draws you in and gives you place to belong and to escape into. And that is a WONDERFUL thing, those that can write like that are blessed above most.

But it bears mentioning that most fiction is based on reality. At least at some point.

I've met Anne Rice two or three times, although I am just one of the masses to her. Anne lost her daughter to leukemia at a very young age. She didn't know what to do with her life, so she went to a writing workshop. Then she channeled her sorrow by writing "Interview With A Vampire". She has said on record that Claudia and Louis represented her daughter and her. Vampires are blood. Michelle died of leukemia.

So, Anne Rice writes cathartically in fiction. She puts her pain in place allegorically. I can't. I never will be able to do that. I am not that blessed or creative. Also, if people deserve recognition for saving lives or sanity, why cloak them in the anonymity of a character? That's how I see this whole thing. I saw myself in Rowan, but I could just as well have seen myself in Lestat or even Stan Rice if I'd really worked hard at it. I wanted someone to believe in, I just didn't know it could be me. So I became Rowan or Scarlett or Catherine or any of the heroines I've loved. And the trust that I had in Anne Rice for allowing me to be Rowan is unbroken.

But for me, as a writer, that's not where I am in my life. I've been alive for awhile, and life doesn't have pretty endings. It's the wonder and joy we pick up along the way that makes it worth living. I can't make up stories when the stories are already there. The uniqueness that is all of us, why hide our freak flags? LOL! I don't want anyone to have to work hard to hear what I'm saying. I want people to know they've made a difference in my life. That's really all I am doing. When I'm gone, would they know how much that one thing meant to me? Doubtful …. I really do believe that coming straight from the heart means the most.

And I am pretty sure I have not met everyone who reads this personally. Which, by the way, I greatly appreciate. I am humbled by the number of "unique" reads. Each and EVERY one of you is giving me a gift, even if you don't like what I'm saying.

So, my self-doubt is now banished because I made you sit and listen. I honestly don't see this blog as just about me. And even if I did, guess what – I'm not going to apologize for being selfish about pursuing something I've dreamt about. There's ego attached to everything we do. But while I have no clue where or how this will evolve, I do know that every keystroke I put out publicly is heartfelt.

If one story brings one smile, or one tear, or even a snarky remark, I've changed something. That is a powerful responsibility my friends. And not something I take lightly.

Golf Balls

My bucket list is always expanding. I hope that always remains so. My bucket list has been emancipating for me. It may contain silly things, but everything is a little challenge to myself: "c'mon kiddo, let's see you make yourself happy. Bet you can't do it. Double dog dare you!" **My bucket list doesn't contain life changing decisions to make, it contains things that help me make life changing decisions.** It builds confidence in me, yes; but moreover it makes me _happy_. We've all heard that word, right?

I know, it's a scary one. Because it means confronting yourself in the present and dealing with you. Lemme tell you. If you can do this, truthfully, you will be happy. I'm learning this verrrrrry slowly, but I'm finally headed in the right direction. We all avoid the "in the moment" us. Know why? Because it is too complicated, too painful, too this or that for us to deal with. So we find other ways to live in our own skin that don't require work. We overcompensate. We're high achievers, we're distracted by cell phones and the internet, we are compulsive workers, eaters, dieters. Or my personal favorite, we're friend hoarders. You know, the moment when you'd like to tell someone the truth but you don't because you are afraid you'll hurt their feelings and they will drop you from their emotional friends list? *sob*

Nope, lemme tell you. You get back as much as you give. Not just to other people, but to you. My life has changed substantially in the past two weeks. I am not afraid anymore. I was afraid of change, of anger, of unhappiness … and then I _finally_ realized that that was exactly what I was living. I took a step out of the box (unplanned, and probably a result of years of unhappiness) and demanded respect. If you give it to me, I will surely give it back to you. And guess what? After many many years, I am learning to be emotionally free. There aren't words for me to describe to you how my life has changed. When you can accept that you are human, that you are entitled to your feelings, and that no one (and I mean no one) is more important than you are, then you start to self-respect yourself. It's not egotistical. It's the truth.

The point of all of this is this: each and every one of us hides behind the immediate in our lives in some fashion. We avoid ourselves, we avoid the hard choices. It's natural to want to do this; I think it's probably normal to want to do this. But help yourself out. No one else is going to, really. Remember, if you are moving in a direction that a friend feels stilted in, they may resent it without even knowing about it. You can't change anyone else, but you can confront and change yourself.

Make a bucket list of things you want to do. And do them. DO them. And when you're doing them, confront yourself and say "hey self! WTH? I'm having a blast. We should do more things like this." I think my first big bucket list was being an extra in a movie in Baltimore. It was amazing, inexpensive (I even got paid for it), and I have so many memories from it. The icing on the cake was it was an experience I shared with my son. Score! Eight hours of fun, and I took my first step out of the box.

I think you'll find that the more you nurture yourself, truly CARE about yourself, the easier it becomes to make and accept changes. I'm far from being a spiritual guru, but I can say from experience that grounding yourself, finding yourself, making changes that better yourself FOR yourself is emancipating. How long has it been since you jumped out of bed (other than to avoid a grumpy spouse, urinating dog, meowing cat, or crying baby) feeling like the day was yours to own? Think about that. Getting happy is win/win. Trust me.

Please remember this as well. As selfish as it might make you feel to look out for yourself, I guarantee that you and your spiritual team are the only ones really "there for you". You are your own best friend, you can trust you to keep your secrets, and be there for you. And 99 times out of 100, the advice you get from you, is the best for you. Be strong enough to act on your best friend's advice.

Off to use 6,459 golf balls for 18 holes, and then to spend time with one of the gentlest, kindest people I've had the pleasure to know. Being with her is a balm for me.

Peace!

Letting my fingers do the walkin ...

You have to be old to get that title. It's when yellow pages were relevant. So I'm letting the younger folks off the hook on that.

What I mean is that this is stream of consciousness today. My weekend hasn't gone at all as I planned, and while I missed doing some things I really wanted to do, there will be a next time. Nothing is wrong .. in fact .. everything is more than okay. I had a terrible headache yesterday, probably the result of spring bursting forth with allergens (I am not complaining!), so I've been more quiet than I anticipated. So .. I also started a new novel last night. Might be one of the best I've read yet, it's called "The Collector of Dying Breaths". It's very Anne and Christopher Rice-ish, and very entertaining. I've had trouble putting it down. No. That's not quite true. I read myself to sleep after ten pages. Nevertheless, it has pushed me. And here is where the randomness comes in.

I don't remember where I saw the recommendation for this book, whether it came in email via Amazon, or was on Anne or Christopher's FB page .. don't know, don't care. Just know it was brought to my attention. The book has claimed me as few have in the past. That makes it a keeper for me. It makes me want to read it. It makes me want to turn the page (or electronic page as the case may be). Score.

My answer. Almost. I'm going to sideline a bit here, because I think it's important to share so you understand what I'm saying. I am a spiritual person, I am a Christian. I do not enjoy organized religion because of the control it can exert if it chooses. I don't recall that being the case in my growing up years, but .. it matters not. I feel that I have a very close relationship with the holiest and highest authority. I call him God. And the Blessed Mother Mary. And a host of angelic and spirt friends and guides. This is what I believe. I don't ask you to share that belief, I don't ask you to try to understand that belief, and I respect what your belief is as I expect you to respect mine. But, for the framework of this conversation, that is where I'm coming from.

This "gang" that I hang out with in my head and heart have been very good to me over the years. They have quite literally saved my life, and kept me sane (to whatever degree you consider me sane). Their love, patience, and guidance have finally brought me to a place where I can begin to relax, feel that love inside of me, and grow as a person. I cannot begin to tell you how much balm that is to these old bones.

I cannot even begin to explain to you where they have brought me, the excitement about the future, the "I can do" attitude that in the past was a self-deprecating bowl of jello. I still wrestle with faith in myself, and I always will. But my gang is working overtime to keep me on a path that I want and deserve. My gratitude is boundless.

So back to the book I am reading. A page turner. Engrossing. Easy to read. Characters are believable and make you want to guess where they are going. The storyline is so bizarre that it's almost impossible to belief that humans would give it credence. I started the book believing the book's premise ridiculous. I now think I could be wrong, and so I am a sucker set up for however it ends. Which makes this a GREAT read for me.

I needed a GREAT read. I am going back and reading through some of the great and enduring "masterpieces" of American literature. So much can be learned by doing so. Technique, quality, style, rhythum, story components. I struggle with it.

I feel like I have something inside that needs to be free, but I don't know what it is. I'm being perfectly honest here. I think I have what it takes to put words on paper, but what needs to go on paper is elusive. I feel boxed in, frightened by those who have gone before. Afraid I'll miss the message, if you get what I'm saying.

So, I am relying on my gang for help. And they came through in a big way for me this morning. I found messages all over the place, not the least of which I found in my email. I don't get messages about re-tweets from Twitter, EVER. I only get account messages. I got the below this morning. Nothing, my friends, is coincidence. Nothing. George Eliot? You know George is really Mary Ann Evans - a woman who wrote under a male name so that people would read?? I don't have to do that. But the message is loud and clear.

And so the priority becomes finishing this new book I'm reading. I absolutely believe the answer is in there. Not in it's story. In my story. I believe the gang is showing me that I can do it. And not in the way that I thought I would. So .. I will let them lead. I will set my stubborness on the back burner and be receptive for a change. I'll stop demanding proof or an answer and start listening for the guidance. They're talking, and now I'm listening.

I've much, MUCH to be grateful in my life. Mostly, I'm grateful I'm where I am right now. I don't even wish that this feeling had come years ago. I'm pretty sure I wouldn't have known what to do with it, and wasted it. Now it's all coming together.

Man, this is just the best. I am so happy. I am so grateful. I am evolving.

My babies .. my friends

friend

noun

1. a person attached to another by feelings of affection or personal regard.

2. a person who gives **assistance;** supporter

3. a person who is on good terms with another; a person who is not hostile

The past two days have been very trying for me.

I am a simple person. I'm not impressed by wealth. I don't care what one's educational level is. I care only that people are genuine. There have been very few in my life that I haven't liked. Even now, those that I hurt or hurt me, I still have feelings of fondness for. I may not want to revisit the relationship, but I hold no grudge. I am an atypical Scorpio. I am often more wounded than I wound. And sometimes I hurt myself more than anyone else could. But, I have learned to rise from the ashes if I have to.

Thing is, rising above adversity or illness or soul pain is pretty difficult to do without a friend. I don't know where I would be in my life had I not been graced with some wonderful people who picked me up and helped me back to my feet, or who danced on tables with me, singing "Mony Mony" at the top of our lungs. Each and every one of those I call friend are dear to me, and each and every one of them are special and unique in their own way. I love them all.

But tonight, I single out two people who I've known a relatively short time but who have impacted my life as few others

157

have. The three of us "grew up" together at work. Sometimes I've been a mother figure to them, sometimes I've been a friend figure to them, and sometimes I've been a real major pain in the ass to them, but they have never ever turned their back on me – even when it might have been expedient to do so.

Six years ago in September I began working in Charles Town. I was a beat up woman, having spent years in the belly of the shark doing law in the DC/Montgomery/Frederick arena. I had absolutely no experience in being an Admissions Rep, but the blessed angel that is Jess Jackson, encouraged me to apply. I did, and I interviewed with Terry Grant and Yoci Deal. I'm not sure what they saw in me, but I was offered the job and I accepted. I have not regretted that decision one time, though I have had my moments of frustration. Terry is not only my "boss", but my friend. And I have not yet crafted how to immortalize her in my blog. But when I met her, I knew I wanted to be part of this team.

Two of the young (and I mean these folks are my kids' ages) people that I met in our small shop (at that time, maybe 20 of us?) were Alisa and Jason. Alisa is a willowy powerhouse, with the energy, enthusiasm, intelligence, and heart of the Spartan 300. Jason was a curly topped, barefoot, compassionate young man who took pity on the old lady and let her have his parking permit because there were no more left for her to have. I think he worried I wouldn't make it from the parking lot, let alone having to walk from the free spaces. These two younguns became like my own.

Over the six years that we have worked together, I have watched them grow into even more wonderful people than they were. Jason, who was going to give the job a year, decided to make higher education his career, gathering two Masters Degrees and working on a PhD right now, and has accepted a job with Harvard. I can only cry over this because I am so damn proud of him.

Alisa surged creatively in the department, becoming the one person we all wanted to be when we grew up, earned her Master's Degree in a year, rather than two – all the while providing an incredibly secure and happy home environment for her husband, two children, and extended family. Soccer mom doesn't even begin to cover it. But more than anything, Alisa's intelligence, her doggedness, her desire to even the playing field has propelled her to the top spot in her department, under Jason. To say that these two young people grabbed life with both hands and worked their asses off to be the best that they could be is an understatement. To say that they did this without losing the essence of who they are is the highest compliment I can pay them. Too often we see folks "ascend" the corporate ladder and either lose or compromise themselves along the way. These two young people did not. Stubborn brats – how much do I love you both?

I can't tell you the handholding that has gone on in our relationship. Not me holding theirs … them holding mine. Helping and supporting me on a day to day basis when I felt that I was circling the drain, these two held me up and kept my life jacket on. What they have done for me, I can never repay.

We've had our differences, especially Jason and I. The argument in the Turf was epic. Lisa fortunately missed that one. But what it all has ever come down to was caring. The belief in each other, even if it was a rolling their eyes moment at me.

And that's how it has been for me for six years. I always knew that no matter what happened, fundamentally we had each other's backs. It is, without a doubt, one of the most giving and less stressful relationships I've ever had because they have never needed anything from me, except my friendship. There are no games. And they have given me more than they know.

Now, things are changing. Not between us, but in our circumstances. Jason is leaving for Cambridge, and Alisa is changing departments at work. This will result in a physical distance we have never had. I am heartbroken. Happy but heartbroken. Choices made by one affects all, and life is never static. I have tried very hard not to make these changes about myself, and to be joyful, and to celebrate the absolute amazing opportunities presented, but I am weak. My heart hurts even as I realize that they both have grown into amazing people with golden futures – and what more could a "mother" ask for.

I want them to know that they are loved, and appreciated, and that I am so very grateful our paths crossed. No matter what the future brings, they will both be in my heart and soul forever.

Pain be Gone!

Yeah, this month has been a tough one. Astrologically predicted, of course, but nevertheless difficult to deal with. Happy, sad, pissed, discouraged, elated .. it's all there in a few action packed days. But. The one thing that I always forget is that it's <u>behind</u> me. Today isn't going to happen again unless I'm Bill Murray in Groundhog Day, and there may well be a day in the future when I wish I could go back to today, crappy as it may have been. So maybe it wasn't that bad after all.

It's like childbirth. God, or perhaps just our own memory, is very kind in removing the actual memory of the pain, or else we would probably be a one and done kind of species. It's not a fun experience, and I don't care how you wrap it. I've yet to find anyone who said it was. And if they did, I'd smack them for lying to my face. Yet, those who have done it more than once never remember the discomfort as anything other than an unformed memory - "man, it really hurt" ... "but I don't really remember where or how".

And so that's kind of where I am about today. It really hurt but I don't know where or how. And I don't want this to be a wasted day. I don't want it to be a throwaway. I don't have THAT many days left in the large scheme of things, so I gotta make them count.

So, why'd it hurt? Because people I love are hurting. Because hard and tough decisions are having to be made. Because people I respect and admire are having to look inward to find strength in situations they never thought they'd encounter. They have no choice. And I can't help them. I can't do anything but listen and be there.

This is not a new story, nor is it one I own exclusively. We've all been there. I'm not crying in my beer. What I am trying to do is pluck something out to hold onto from the ruins of the day.

And I know what it is. I sent a friend a small gift. A Carpenters CD. It made him smile. I could feel it through his e-mail. And that smile takes me through the ruins of the day because someone was happy about something in the midst of the chaos that was my day today. His smile was my island. My safe spot. My reassurance that tomorrow will be better. That our lives are more important than the instant we live in.

I know alot of people are struggling right now. Decisions to make, changes to live with. I am neither affected nor unaffected. Yet my heart goes out to all, even as I wonder what will become of me. So, from a crappy day comes this: love. Friendship. Honesty. Giving. Not a bad take today, not at all.

Kahlil Gibran said it best - "Friendship is always a sweet responsibility, not an opportunity."

So I take from today a sweet responsibility to all those I love out of a crappy day. If you need me, I am here.

Easter Eyes

Ladies and Gentlemen, I am doing my Easter ramblings today instead of tomorrow because I am taking the day to spend with family. I've written this post a million times in my head and heart – now if only I can commit to paper what is there. Please bear with me.

I know that some reading don't share my Christian beliefs, and that is totally fine with me. We are all here to do our own thing, and as long as you are each happy, that's all that matters. For those who do believe in the meaning of Easter, I wish you nothing but peace tomorrow as you celebrate the Resurrection, the very foundation of our Christian lives. Enjoy your families, your faith, and your knowledge that one died for our sins so that we all can live. God Bless.

On a lighter note, tomorrow is 4/20 ... I can only imagine the cha ching of the cash registers in Washington and Colorado! Rock on! May your Easter eggs glitter while they do the chicken dance!

Now. To me. There is enormous significance to the fact that April 20th falls on Easter this year. One literal year ago today, on Saturday, April 20, 2013, I went blind in my right eye. There was little warning, and there was no way to prevent it. My age and my myopia combined to cause my retina to detach to a degree of 90%. That meant that, by the mid-afternoon of this day last year, I could see only a thin white strip out of my right eye, and only if I looked straight up at the ceiling. Otherwise, I had no sight in that eye. Pretty shocking way to spend a spring Saturday.

I spent most of the day in the emergency room at Johns Hopkins (Hopkins plays such a huge role in my life). There were 3 other eye-related injuries that day (an unusual number according to the staff), and so I waited almost six hours to see a doctor.

During those six hours, my husband sat with me as I slowly, without pain or discomfort, went blind in that eye. And there was nothing we could do to stop it. We were at the Wilmer Eye Clinic, one of the top five places in perhaps the entire world to be for an eye issue. I couldn't have been in a better place, but even that did not prevent me from going blind.

When I was finally able to see the doctor, around 4:00 p.m., I was told to lie still, and the lights were turned off in the room. This was to prevent movement and light in a hope to stop the progress of the detachment. After the initial diagnosis was confirmed, things kicked into a high gear. A team was called in, including a top surgeon in the department. It was their Saturday off. The Institute's outpatient surgery _building_, not suite, not room, the entire building, was opened for me. Understand that this included calling in everyone from nurses and nesthesiologists to security guys because the building had been shut down for the weekend.

I was told that they would attempt to re-attach my retina. I'm not going to go into detail about the surgery because frankly, unlike childbirth, every step of this journey is burnt into my cellular structure, and I do remember the pain. Believe me, and my friends can confirm this, I never EVER used "I hate that so much I could stick pins in my eyes" after my surgery because that is, indeed, what happened. Be careful what you ask for!

I was taken into surgery around 9:00 p.m. that night. Ian and Michelle (my loves) came to stay with Dave. They were in a huge waiting room with only a security guard. All the staff was attending to me in the surgical suite. They could not know what was happening. Plus, the surgery was projected to go an hour. It stretched to three, and there was no one to tell my family why. I cannot imagine what they went through. I can only tell you that had they not been there, I don't know how strong I would have been.

In a nutshell, the surgery was success. I have gazillions of stories about it, but that is not what I am writing today. That wonderful team of professionals saved my right eye when it was gone. Yes, they were trained to do what they did, but I believe with my whole heart that God guided their hands. That my spiritual gang was with me the entire time, and that it was a lesson for me, and one that I have taken to heart.

And yes, Dave, Ian and Michelle were finally told that all was well, and it was explained to them what took so long. Suffice to say that problems were encountered during surgery and dealt with. My heart hurt for the three of them to have been left alone to wonder how our lives would be changing, and I know that the fear they felt for me was very real and painful.

To underscore the significance of placement of people in our lives, the surgeon who operated on me left Hopkins two months later to go into private practice down South. I cut that one really close.

My point here is this: nothing in our lives is coincidental or random. Not the people, not the events, not the timing. Sometimes it is really hard to understand the why of things, and that's when I fall back so hard on my faith.

And that is why this year, the fact that Easter falls on the one year anniversary of my regaining my sight, is so very meaningful for me. Faith. What a tiny word for such a huge gift. I will tell you now that only briefly did I feel fear. I can't explain why, but in my heart, I knew that regardless of the outcome, I would be okay. I didn't feel alone in the operating room, or in the weeks that came afterward with exceptionally painful follow up treatment. My gang was with me.

To say that my family and friends were with me 1000% percent is an understatement, and I will never be able to thank all of you for all that you gave me. Hope, love, comfort. Even those at a distance who sent messages. Every single one of you contributed to my recovery, and I thank you from the bottom of my heart.

But the team in the operating room with me, the one I couldn't see but knew with certainty was there, re-gifted me with something I took for granted. And THAT is my Easter celebration this year. A genuine renewal of faith, a genuine and most sincere thank you to God – both for the great sacrifice made by him for me (and those who believe), as well as the second chance I was given.

I am spending tomorrow outside. I want to see spring, the colors, the flowers .. everything. I no longer take any of that for granted, and I don't want you to do that either. Please know that you are loved, beyond any love we flawed humans can understand, and that your steps aren't taken alone.

Happy Easter everyone! May your Easter eggs roll, and your serenity rock!

Peace.

The Easter Story – an alternate version

What a beautiful day today! Loved my walk (the donut story will be told at another time), took pictures of spring unfolding here in Brunswick, celebrated the spirituality of the day and the season. Also cleaned and did laundry. Hey. Some things have to be done no matter how grateful you are for all the spiritual gifts you've been given. Those clothes aren't gonna wash themselves!

So, it's been a full, busy day – not the one I expected or planned – but a very nice one anyway. Except, of course, for the guy who let his dog pee and poop all over my yard with no "doggie bag" to clean up with. Really annoyed me. Just because there is a hydrant in the yard doesn't mean it's fair game to give offerings to the poop gods. Oh well …

I'm in a story telling kind of mood today. I hope none of the peeps I tell on get upset, but if they do, I'm prettttty sure it's not the first time they will have been upset with me ….

Easter brings back a memory that is, without a doubt, one of the most perfect memories I have. No matter how much time elapses, it is as clear as bell – both the situation and my reaction to it. There was a time when both my bestie Kim and I were single mothers. Actually, there was a lot of time when that was true. Kim's daughter Holland, and my daughter, Betsy, had been joined at the hip since meeting in Montessori pre-school. They were an absolute delight, and the stories from their growing up sustain me. It also makes me exceptionally proud to see the women they have grown into. Different from each other, but both sincere and happy women. A good thing.

So when Holland and Betsy were … oh I think about 5 or so, Kim and I decided that we should take them to Sunday Easter service. Holl was always the more outgoing of the two, Betsy more reserved. So we dress them up, and we go to church. It was a beautiful service, and when it was time for the children's sermon, the minister asked all the children to come up to the altar so he could talk with them about the meaning of Easter. Holland was a beautiful, angelic child .. and full of life. She didn't hesitate for a moment, and up she went. Betsy chose not to go. All good on both counts. The minister didn't hesitate to scoop Holland up on his lap as he sat in the Chancel. So she sat, with the other children scattered at their feet.

The minister walked them through Palm Sunday and through Jesus's hearing before Pilate. The children were enraptured, Holland not the least of them. Her eyes grew larger and larger as the minister described the pain and suffering that Christ suffered. The minister then asked the children if they knew what had then happened to Christ, and Holland, with all the innocence of small child, and the drama of Bette Davis, drew her little hand across her throat and shouted "and then they SLIIIIIIIIT his throat!".

I looked at Kim sitting next to me, and thought (not for the first time) that if the earth could swallow us up at that exact moment, we would die happy women. Betsy was aghast that the story ended that way, and Kim's look of stunned horror is, to this day, ingrained in my memory.

The minister was a good sport about it (what choice did he really have??) and the fact that Holland was so adorable helped immensely. He laughed and said "no, no .. that's not exactly what happened, but it's a good guess." Holland looked totally indignant that the story didn't end the way she planned. The minister finished the story, blessed the children, and they all went back to their seats. I have never heard Kim sing a closing hymn with such gusto! And, I think we may have left the church before the last chorus of "I Know That My Redeemer Liveth".

It is one of the many moments in parenthood where you it is too precious, too precocious, too original to not appreciate. We laughed so hard on the way home, and the girls had no clue why we were laughing so hard tears were streaming down our faces.

But, oh there was such love. We struggled as Moms to do the right thing. Our girls were the most precious things in our lives. We both eventually ended up marrying again and bearing sons. But for awhile, it really was just the four of us. I'm not sure I can speak of a time in my life when there was such a precious, uncomplicated time. Our girls were our lives. Kim and I were different mothers, she was a bit stricter (okay, a LOT stricter) than I was, so we offset each other's parenting style.

And the girls. Oh my goodness. Both so beautiful, so happy, so in love with each other and the worlds they created together. Holland just as sassy as she could be, Betsy dry and sarcastic. Holland very much a girl's girl, Betsy content to wear the same outfit every day (provided it was clean). I knew that if Betsy stayed with Kim, that I would never need worry about her safety; and vice versa with Holland and I. The girls could entertain themselves for hours – I will never forget the time I found them both standing in the kitty litter box pretending they were at the beach. Or the night I wrote in red lipstick on the mirror "Bloody Mary was here" and then hid to hear their reaction. Oh my, Holland's very soprano voice was screaming "oh no oh no oh no oh no" and Betsy's very alto voice calmly saying "I told you we shouldn't have said her name". Totally priceless.

Now, they are 29. Holland turned 29 on April 2 and shortly thereafter gave birth to her and her husband Joe's second child, son Vincent. Betsy will turn 29 in August, and she lives in her own home, with her three dogs who are her children. Very different lives yet not so unexpected while watching them grow up. So very proud of both of them.

And Kim, what can I say? For 25-26 years now we've beaten each other up, thrown pots and pans at each other, I even sued her. We fight like the sisters that we are. Have we always been good to the other? No. Have we always put the other's interests before our own? No. But just as Betsy and Holland grew, so did we. Our relationship isn't perfect, by any means, but I'd have it no other way. When the real chips were down, it was me and Kim against the world.

I truly wouldn't have had it any other way.

Ahhhh .. a good day indeed when your memories make you smile!

Hail Caesar Salad

Forcing myself to write tonight. I need to do it every day, but for a number of reasons, just not feeling it tonight. A gift arrived for me at work today, but I was at the doctor, so I am very anxious to get to work to open it tomorrow. It is a book on Michelangelo. I do love the Renaissance period, so I'm totally going to enjoy this.

I would love to go visit Greece and Italy. I'm not so much on Europe. Probably because I think I've been there before, but that's another subject for another day. But I would love to go and _touch_ the history of Greece and Italy. I can't even imagine what touching the Coliseum would be like. The Sistine Chapel. The thousands of years of history there. Athens. The Mediterranean. That's my dream trip. The Greek Islands. So beautiful. Such a graceful way of life. Rome.

ROME.

I'm not sure there is a more powerful historical word, except for God.

[Editors note: Okay, now I also want to go to Egypt and see where Cleopatra, Antony, and Caesar trysted. You know really, I love rock, but our "Layla" trio (Eric, George and Patti) got NOTHING on these guys (although it IS a kick ass song and I don't recall a song called "Cleo" coming out of that original mess). This is 100% Bell Bottom Blues" right here. Good grief. Who kills themselves with a snake? Wow. Just wow. And with full make up on? Holy crap. That's serious intention right there. But, better that I guess than dragged through the streets of Rome in a cage looking like crap. And who knows what ole Jules would have done with her. Et tu Brute? Your turn.]

Ah the debauchery of Rome. I like how that which is outlawed or scorned or branded .... umm ... bad ... today was not only common practice back then, but ... well ... artistically celebrated. Here we call it porn. We find pictures of women "with" minotaurs in a cave now, it's worth millions. Go figure. Does that mean that "Deep Throat" will be considered a work of art in the future. God I hope not. At least until they take it out of the Super 8 format. But I digress.

Yes, yes .. everyone agrees that if the United States doesn't study the rise and fall of the Roman Empire, we will go down in a hail of fiery arrows. That we (and Hitler's Germany) are the only countries since Rome to salute by pounding on our chests or something. I wasn't paying attention. But, there is something to be said by comparison. One word.

Arrogance.

The Romans started out being really really smart by listening to the Greeks (who had their own issues with sexuality and animals and stuff, but it was cool) and then they just kept busting peoples' chops, taking their country, planting flags all over the place and VOILA. The Roman Empire. Here are all these poor countries, just doing their thing, maybe having a little fight amongst themselves, and what happens? The dudes in the red outfits with outrageous feathery helmets come in, cut their heads off, burn their huts, take their women and chickens (their only commodities) and claim their country. Then they send people to the country to 'govern' it, which generally meant tax the crap out of the children, since everyone else was dead or bartered off, and they spent all day walking around in circles making grain like Conan the Barbarian. Then, the worker bees would get tired of being taxed, and they would revolt. And then they would get their country back to themselves. Or have their heads put on spikes.

Sound familiar to anyone? I think we (as Americans) started out on the right foot, tea party and all that, but dear God, is there any group of people on the face of the planet that the United States hasn't pissed on? Let's just start with Native Americans and work on down.

Arrogance.

Yes, this is one of those things that angers me. I wish I had been a Druid (maybe I was. Make note to find out) ... at least they were cool. They didn't try to take over people's lands, or tell them what to think, or what they could or could not do, or how they should live, or even what tea they should drink. All they did was grow long hair, dress oddly, meditate, chant, and possibly offer up human sacrifices (does anyone see a pattern here? I don't know their thoughts on sex, so I can't really 100% compare this to the '60s, but damn close! I can't prove the human sacrifice thing either.) BTW, this tidbit comes from Caesar himself who spent some time with the Druids, and actually wrote the first recorded history of them. Busy Boy. Chant, conquer, kill, have sex, chant, conquer, kill, have sex. Now there's a day to be proud of! A little like the Maharishi poisons everyone's tea.

Oh. And the Druids did build henges. Whatever a henge is (attribution: Eddie Izzard)

So ... Roman Empire ..... United States ..... Roman Empire .... United States.

That makes my head hurt. I think I will go back and review some of the history of the Roman Empire so I can determine exactly which era of the Empire the US stands in right now - you know, which Caesar's reign are we in, or is Obama actually Caligula? [I just gave the right a new quote. Let's see if it makes Fox!] Inquiring minds wants to know. And, I want to indulge in the debaucheries before it's too late.

Although, Washington and Colorado are on the right track. Some say Sodom and Gommorah. I say "right on!"

Courage

According to the stats on my website (the few I actually understand), the average read time on my blog is about 30 seconds or so. So, fair warning. Today's post may require a bit more than 30 seconds to read. And, it could make you uncomfortable. Or, you might see yourself in it. You may not even understand it, or care. But this post is as real as it's going to get, at least in my world.

I am a 59 year old, college educated, fairly intuitive, outgoing, mother of two. My children are wonderful creatures who, despite my influence, have managed to develop into balanced, happy humans. I have a great job with folks I love. I live in a home that I love and that is as quirky as I am. I am blessed to have friends that I love and who love me. I have everything that most people want.

I am also the victim of domestic abuse

I have never been physically assaulted. Part of me wishes I had – perhaps I would have been able to accept the truth by having a black eye or broken limb. Non-physical domestic abuse is, to me, far more insidious. It is silent, deep reaching, scarring. It is your screaming and screaming in a space inside where no one can hear or help you. It is longing to know what is wrong with you, what you did to incur this punishment, and it is not being able to admit to yourself that you need help. It is hiding behind a façade of normalcy. It is shame. Deep shame.

I met my husband about 15 years ago. I was single, he was not. That was not an option for me. He became single, and we got married. From the beginning, I knew something was very wrong. But, as I am finding out, I was the perfect candidate for a domestic violence situation - just ripe for the picking. My life, to that point, was a series of hits and misses, successes and failures. I was not proud of myself – quite the opposite – and I was looking for a way to validate myself. I saw my husband as a successful man, arrogant but in an endearing way, and I truly believed I was lucky that he saw something in the person that I was. Instant validation for me.

And so it began. His consuming jealousy, need for control, the sudden rages. We joined a bowling league with friends, and if I even spoke to one of my teammates who was male, the anger and sulking began. Our first New Year's Eve together, we attended a party at a club we belonged to. A close friend of ours (male) gave me a big hug and picked me up off the ground. I was punished verbally because I allowed another man to touch me. I was at my most vulnerable then. I needed to be wanted and to be loved. My husband already had a leg up just on that score. He convinced me. I believed him. I believed that I was evil, and wanton, and wicked. It was all my fault, everything. When one of the kids left just a smidge of Coke in the bottle, it was thrown across the room in a fit of anger … my son eating the last wing in a bucket from KFC resulted in a major tantrum. The stakes became higher. Now, it wasn't just about me. It was about my children as well. How easy was this? What mother wouldn't sacrifice her pride or anything else to protect her kids? But was that what I was doing? Or would a mother remove her kids from the situation?

We would go out for the evening and a male would speak to me. I paid dearly for that on the ride home, and when we got home, my seven year old son would be awakened to be told his mother was a whore. The police were called during a drunken rage, and I had to call a friend to come get my daughter. One night, I drove to a friend's house and hid in their bushes to escape the anger. Probably the worst? Waking up in the middle of the night to see him standing, silently, in the dark at the foot of the bed staring at me. No talking. At all.

176

All of this? In the first two years of this relationship. A relationship I remain in today. Why? Why?

I have no excuse. I can never make enough apologies to my children, my friends .. His anger never touched them, I protected them .. but in doing so, I lost their respect, and my respect for myself. And so it continued. I can't even begin to describe the feelings of fear and anxiety. I feel them now as I write, and I know there is no way to convey them to you. All I wanted was a home and family ... a "normal" life. I was ready to sacrifice everything I was for that. Until I realized I had gained nothing and stood to lose everything.

Over the years, I had friends reach out to me, try to intervene. Try to get me to see what it was I was allowing to happen. I allowed dear friendships to be lost because of my husband. I walked away from people who cared because they dared to try to make me see the truth. I slapped my own daughter for asking me why I let him do this to me. That, my friends, is a continuing pattern of domestic violence. There simply is no sugarcoating that.

This doesn't happen in my upper middle class life. This is not how I was raised. What the hell is happening to me? That became my mantra, and I fell further and further down the rabbit hole. My son grew up loving this man as his stepdad. To this day, they are still close. But my son has had to speak up for me, I didn't have the nuts to do it. My son did. And it made things better for a night. But then the cycle started again.

When I went to work in Charles Town, I met the most remarkable group of people. I know I've ranted and raved about them before, but they are amazing. Going old school, Terry .. Jason .. Alisa ... people who didn't know my past, didn't know my life, and didn't care. They just ... get ready for this ... liked me. Over the years, our group expanded, and I met and became friends with more and more folks, until I was able to finally recognize that it was ME that they liked, and I didn't have to DO anything for them to like me. Only God knows how much this has meant in my life because I do not have the words. And those of you know who you are .. Trudy, Shandi, Jess, Natalie, Alyson, Matt, Jennifer, Laura, Kevie, Corinne, Mary P., Yoci, Kristina ... so many of you who showed me the way back. Just cannot thank you enough for the years of love you have shared with me (okay, maybe not in Kristina's case – I don't wanna speak for her). They strengthened me. They bolstered me. NOT by tearing down anything, but with love. And concern. They brought me back to life.

Still, even with support, it has taken six years for my personal rebuilding to begin. Six more years that I walked on eggshells, that I was afraid of bringing people to my home, or taking my husband out to meet friends. One night, to celebrate a friend's birthday, we went out to dinner. It was one of the worst nights of my life. To be with these folks I loved so dearly, and for my husband to embarrass me, belittle me, and speak down to my friends as he did. It was mortifying. NOT because of his actions as much as my inability to change. I was inert.

I moved out twice between then and now – neither stuck. There are a myriad of reasons for that. Practical reasons, and stupid reasons. But the plan wasn't good. BTW, did you know – statistically, it takes a victim of domestic abuse _seven_ attempts to break free ... if they ever do.

Finally, a month ago. I emotionally broke free. The circumstances are not important except that it was a "normal" bullying situation, but this time I found my voice. I told him that I would not be spoken to or treated like that again. I don't know where the words came from, I honestly don't. What I do know is that they roared out of me. And that I will never take them back. And I will thank God for giving me that voice until my dying day and then perhaps some.

What has changed? I still live in the same house with him. We still interact daily. The change? Me. I gave him the power to control me, to hurt me, to frighten me, to wound me, and I am scarred. I am blackened inside like a sooty chimney. But for the first time in years, I am alive. I am cleansing myself, with help from my spiritual gang and God. I am accepting who I am, and setting goals for me. I want to stand up and be recognized for me. I want to be proud of me. And .. I'm getting there.

To all of those who suffer in silence, to all who feel words crush their soul, to all who fend off a blow (physically or emotionally), I offer my love and my empathy. So many times I'd watch shows where women were physically abused and I'd remark that they must not have much self-esteem if they couldn't walk away from that. And then I would realize that I was a hypocrite. Because self-esteem, that most fragile of butterflies, is the key, domestic abuse is the hardest fight to fight. Please. Don't suffer in silence. Don't wait for an answer. Seek the answers for yourself and take advantage of resources available to you. Don't stay in things "for the kids". Ask yourself if you would be happy watching your own child live as you do. These aren't easy questions, and believe me, the answers are even more difficult.

But you can do it. I did it. Or, rather, I am doing it. Every day presents a new set of challenges. I can't predict how it will all end. In our situation, there are practicalities of life that need to be considered. But they are minor compared to my peace of mind and sense of self.

This story isn't over. But at least I now have a sense of direction rather than a sense of dread.

Do we care?

I went to visit my daughter after work today. She scared the bejesus out of me before lunch (I still worry about her at 29, yes!) because she got hit with a sudden bad tummy and sweats. I asked her if she wanted me to come down, and she said no. She was fine. Then about half an hour before I was to leave, I got a text asking me to bring her some McDonalds fries. There's my WTF moment for the day. When I called her on that, she said "well. A girl's gotta eat." In some weird way, I get that. So, I took her what she asked for, spent some time with her and her pups and now, I am home again, in front of the monitor. I miss her already.

Driving to her house, I passed a large pawn shop. We all know that pawn shops are like hookers – always been around, always will be around because they serve a need. I'm not being judgmental here at all, believe me. I've had to take things to a pawn shop to sell in order to make ends meet before. BUT, as I drove past this large shop, the entire front of the shop, outside, was lined with bicycles. Kids' bikes. All sizes. Now, I get that kids outgrow bikes and I guess pawning one instead of throwing it away, giving it away or donating it is an okay thing, but even with reason shouting that in my ear, I felt hollow when I saw those bikes.

Pink bikes with baskets and streamers, Hot Wheels, 10 speeds, trikes. I felt tears well up, and I had to acknowledge the pain that I felt from seeing this row of maybe 25-30 kids bikes lined up for sale at a pawn shop. And after I got past being teary, I got angry. What kind of world is this where we have parents pawning their kids' bikes? There are a couple of possibilities. One, they need the money to put food on the table. This, to me, is horrifying and heartbreaking. Or two, they need the money for a vice.. feel free to pick any one. I can't even comment on that because I'll throat punch the monitor [thank you Kaci!].

Now, it's possible the kids outgrew the bikes and they just sold them to the shop. Very possible, so let's eliminate say .. 1/3 of the bikes (I've never known anyone to do this, but I am giving it credibility) ... that's 10 of the 30. That leaves about 20 childrens' bicycles for sale for unknown reasons. I actually think the 1/3 is high. But .. this isn't a research paper. It's a discussion.

How sad is that? Are there 20 kids somewhere who went out to ride their bike and it was gone? If their bike was gone for financial reasons, I can't even bear to think of what they were told. Or the possible toll on the parents.

I was a single mother for awhile, with no support. No problem. Betsy is MY daughter, and I took responsibility for her. Some good decisions, some bad ones. But she's doing pretty damn well right now. I never made a bundle, but I could pay the bills. It was a narrow margin though, and sometimes bills were passed over in favor of new school shoes or a present to go to a birthday party. And you know what? The electric and phone were never cut off. But they could have been. I was lucky. And that's all I could think of when I saw those bikes.

I know all parents struggle, but damn if it doesn't seem like they are struggling harder now than they used to. What next? What is going to happen to everyone when the last bike has been pawned? And we wonder why there is crime.

I am not suggesting that all of those bikes were at that pawn shop to put food on someone's table, but given the sheer number of them, I'm willing to bet at least one was. And that's one kid too many whose bike was sold for dinner.

Folks, this is not a 3rd world country I'm talking about, it's the United States of America. Yes, people make mistakes – not everyone is a financial wizard. Not everyone has a high paying job, in fact, not everyone HAS a job. And yet all we can do is throw stones at each other about who is responsible for what. Nothing ever, EVER gets done because we are so busy being righteous.

Please. Consider a random act of kindness. Congress won't. But we can. If we don't help each other, what are we? Seriously. What does that make us? It makes us lazy, undisciplined, selfish, and ready to pass the blame onto someone … anyone .. else.

Reach out. Help someone. You won't believe the difference it will make in their lives. Maybe even in yours. But .. here is the warning … not until you stop patting yourself on the back for helping will you truly be helping. Think about that.

And that row of bikes. Each one had an owner.

Big Bang?

This whole Big Bang theory/Neil Degrasse Tyson stuff has me on edge. Let me tell you why. There is not a doubt in my mind that scientifically the Big Bang occurred. None. We have become so technologically advanced that we, the common folk, probably don't know how technologically advanced we, the world, really are.

I can look at situations multi-generationally 3 times – my Mom, me, and my children. I remember having to help my Mom with the subtraction in her checkbook. When I was in elementary school. And anyone who knows me knows that my Mom was putting herself at great risk if a mathematical process was involved in something I was doing. My point being – that was then, and now .. I hit "reconcile checking" and it's done. We have telescopes pointed at, and recording things, light years (LIGHT YEARS people, not decades) away from us. I always thought medicine was so cool in Star Trek – you just laid there and they ran a scanner over you and found out what was wrong. Umm. Yeah, I had that done not too long ago at Jefferson Memorial in Charles Town.

My point is that yes, scientifically we have progressed to the point where we have made such progress that, before too long, we will be just one huge science experiment. Orwell was on track, but not even close. Things we used to call conspiracy theories (remember soldiers and government workers being injected to test LSD?) turn out to be true. So, hey .. I'm open to everything. Yep, I think we would be way egotistical to think we are the only viable life forms in the universe. Yep, I think the government has been black opping us for years in ways we will never know. And I guess it's possible that Michael Jackson talked like a man when he was in real life (yep, read that the other day as well).

I have no clue just how advanced we are. I will never know, and frankly, I don't want to know. I've grown up frightened. I don't want to take the Metro, or anything that risks my ability to get out if ricin appears. It seems too easy that our water systems have never been touched. The fact that we've been hit so few times with terrorism is mind boggling. And the truth is that we have science and technology to **_thank_** for all of this. We are protected by science, but we are also decimated by science. It is good to move forward and it is bad to move forward.

All of which brings me to this question: where did the VERY FIRST atom come from? The scientific community is very very good at avoiding that question, and the double speak that comes in response to that question is amazing. No one knows. That's the bottom line. Whether you are an aetheist, agnostic, Christian, Muslim, Jew … no one knows for SURE where that first atom comes from. So, if we even bother with ruminating on this at all, we pick a place to be to answer that question.

I choose to believe that in the beginning, there was God. Call the creator of the universe whatever you want: Muslims call it Allah, Hindus call it Vishnu and Shiva, Sikhs call it Waheguru, and so on. In many religions, it is "the Supreme Being". So, I think it's fair to say that in most religions or spirituality forums, there is a Supreme Being who is responsible for the creation. Nowhere have I ever read that in the beginning there was the Big Bang, closely followed by the creation of a Supreme Being. Now all of this, of course, relates to folks who believe in God, or a Supreme Being. Many do not. Among them: Agnosticism, Apatheism, Atheism, Deism, Henotheism, Ignosticism, Monotheism, Omnism, Panenthaneism, Pantheism, Polytheism, Theism, Transtheism and so on. There are also less popular but nevertheless embraced "religions" of Paganism, Wicca, Satanism, etc. BUT, even in those, we find a Supreme Being.

Now, here is what bothers me. Ron White did a comedy segment (and this may be considered NSFW by some – be warned) about a toilet in a hotel that had a bidet. He used the bidet to clean his butt. He loved the experience. And I laughed really hard, trust me. But then he said "500,000 gay men cannot be wrong". Think about that for a moment.

I've been taught to read things between the lines, to think out of the box, to give alternative thinking its due. I want you to think about what Ron White said.

Is it possible that so MANY of us are wrong? Over centuries and centuries? That those of us with faith in a Supreme Being, and I don't care what you call him/her/it, being our raison d'être are idiots? Can millions of people be WRONG? Or worse - delusional.

Is organized religion all that and a bag of chips? No. Not in my opinion but it gives structure (some would say control) to people's lives. Let me say right here that I believe that extremism of _any_ kind is wrong. Balance is the key to life, and swinging too far on the branch may cause you to fall and break your neck.

The Catholic Church has taken the biggest hit, obviously. It's a shame because the Catholic Church is a beautiful thing. Its rituals, the masses in Latin. It is like touching history. And what happened? It's not cool for men who profess to love God and all mankind to make little boys do those hideous things. Or little girls for that matter, though we hear little about that. What twists our panties so much about this is that .. THESE ARE MEN OF GOD. So, if these are men of God, God must suck.

No. God does not suck.

God sustains us and he gives us choices. Everyone. Hitler had choices. Mother Theresa had choices. I have had choices. Pedophiles have choices. Gays have choices – not what you thought I was gonna say is it? But they do. They can either deny themselves so that they conform to other's misguided ideas or they can bravely step out of the box and be who God intended them to be. We ALL have choices. And you can't thank a hole in the solar system for that. Seriously? A bunch of molten lava and some protein and here we are? Nope. Not buying it.

I've seen too much good and bad, too much hurt and happiness, too much humanity to ever believe anything other than this. In the beginning, God created the heaven and the earth. As my friend Ron said, perhaps we should have had inserted "and then he created the Big Bang" as the next line in the Bible.

But it's not there. If it was meant to be there, it would be. We can rock on with our science, and our technology, and our upward mobility – but how many of us have longed for things to slow down, to go back to where we used to be? That may be one of the prices we pay for science and technology.

But I am not willing to give up my belief that God gave me the gift of life and he trusts me to live up to the challenges. I will never believe that I am simply the result of an abstract one in a bazillion chance in a universe that we know exists beyond anything we can even imagine. I am not dissing those who do, your choices are your own. But I couldn't live my life without faith, without knowing that there was more than this. And not needing a telescope or microscope to prove it.

Just my two cents for today!

Are we going to Scarborough Hall?

So, a return to my Living Legends list …. Today I celebrate a group. A very special group. The kids from Scarborough.

I laugh a bit when I think of the humor I find in my daughter moving at her own speed, until I realize that I did the same thing. I did things my way almost always, and that included higher education. I flunked out of Radford (pffffft) and then wandered my way through Chesapeake College, collected enough credits to get in, and headed off to Towson State University (remember when that was its name?) to finish it up.

My Towson days are a book in and of themselves, but for now I just want to concentrate on my senior year. I transferred in for my junior year, but chose to live off campus. I thought that would be way cooler. It wasn't. I was way out of the real action sphere. So, for my senior year, I consulted with the party gods, and they suggested that I apply for a room in Scarborough Hall. Right on! Score! Scarborough was one of the last (Prettyman being the last, I think?) of the old dorms to go coed.

All the floors except the first were coed. The reason for that, it was a short hall because of all the public space, so only one bathroom. So the first floor was all girls. Guess where they put me? Oh yeah. Not only on the first floor, but in the room next to the RA. Quoi? What is this? He turned out to be really cool, but that's another story.

I had no idea who my roommate would be – I didn't know anyone except the Russian gal I'd shared a hut with off campus. So, I was open to anything. And that is what I got. I don't know if it was because I was a few years older than everyone else, or I look like a softie, or whatever, but my roommate (and her name escapes me) was handicapped. I really don't want to make a big deal about this, except to say that it didn't work out for her, physically, to be in the dorm. I felt really sorry for her, and I wish I could have helped more, but ... she needed more privacy than a dorm affords. She left after two weeks and I had a room to myself! All right then. But .. no.

My next roommate was a gal named Patti. Now. Patti was the antithesis of she who had just vacated. She had a custom made bong that she shared freely. Seriously. Does it get any better? The only problem with Patti was that she also had extreme sinus issues and was congested a lot. So, she bought a humidifier for the room. The result was an environment a bit like a marijuana rainforest. My sheets and pillow case were wet, like hemp drying in the sun. It was like sleeping with your head in bong water. After a couple of months of this, we decided to part ways.

It was during the Patty siege that I met Susan. She lived down the hall from me (having also drawn the short stick for the coed thing ... sorta) ... her roommate's name was Denise. Now this gets complicated, so stay with me. Denise's significant other, Gwen, lived down the hall also. After Gwen and Denise broke up, Gwen became the girlfriend of the guy who had been my significant other for four years. Honestly, you'd think on a campus the size of Towson there'd be more variety or something.

But Susan was different than everyone else. If you think I wear my heart on my sleeve, you've not seen anything. I think that Susan may have the biggest heart and suffered more hurt over her life than most of us, yet she is always smiling, always happy. And dayum, did we have some good times. There was a group of us: a couple of Jims, Tim, Mitch, Cindy, Paul (formerly known as ... well, okay I'll let that one go because I heart him), Gary, Tom, Ed ... the list goes on. OMG. Hal Saxby. Lord have mercy. Remember him? I cannot hear anything but the song "Can't you see?" when I think of Hal. And that dumb stuffed beaver.

Mitch had the thankless job of being our RA (in addition to the one in the room next to me who had a "thing" with my ex-roomie Patti). Wade and Cindy I'd grown up with in Chestertown, Ed was a late arrival to Chestertown, Tom (don't think you're getting away unscathed here .. your day will come!) was an Eastonian. From Maryland. Not the Soviet Union.

So many memories:

Susan filling up her very expensive purse with shrimp from the all you can eat shrimp bar at Beefsteak Charlies (I think?) and forgetting about them for a day or so ….

The National Bank of Squirt. I'll leave this there because only we understand this and it sounds bad.

Mitch writing my sorry ass up for throwing water balloons out of the second floor windows. Seriously? Though to be fair, he did warn me.

Celebrating my 25th birthday. I remember a picture of my unwrapping an album as a gift. Remember that? You always knew it was an album. LOL!

Susan and I lying on the floor in either of our rooms, drunk, wailing to the entirety of "Jesus Christ Superstar". Occasionally we picked parts, but generally it was just all about singing four sides of a double album.

Wade's band playing at the C'town Saloon and all of us hustling butt down for the show. Margaritaville with the refrain that it was "all Kathi's fault" .. tip of the hat there my friend!

Taking all of the pins out of the hinges that held one of the bathroom stalls together so that an unpopular student would have the sides fall in on him.

Vaseline-ing doorknobs (my personal fave was when there were tampons hung on them)

Thursday night "Drink of the Week" night in Galligan's room. I don't know what we paid, but that was the cheapest and best night out ever. I can remember hearing blenders all night.

Skipping down the 2nd floor hall holding Susan's hand. Now, you have to understand that I am a good 6 inches taller and a gazillion pounds heavier than Susan. Susan is the equivalent of a Chihuahua, whereas I am a Bull Mastiff. So, we are skipping down the hall, holding hands (I want to believe with all my heart that we'd had too much to drink) and as we were doing so, someone called my name. So I stopped skipping. Unfortunately, the slingshot effect kicked in and Susan flew into a large hallway trashcan, head first. I know it sounds awful, but I am laughing sooooooo hard!

Preakness infield. Peeing in refrigerator boxes. Craig and Gary and Denise.

John Lennon died. I remember a number of people coming to my room to tell me. I was a couple of years older, and they figured it would mean something. I was sound asleep. Then it felt like a nightmare. I remember going to the memorial service for Lennon in downtown Baltimore.

"Paradise by the Dashboard Light". Never since has that song sounded as good as it did in the basement of Scarborough. Well done you guys!

And one of my all time personal favorites, when Ed and Tom thought it would be hilarious on April Fools Day to prank my new roommate, Elyse, who was from Potomac, MD, and turn everything on her side of the room around backwards. Yeah. She flipped a f'ing nut on her books. She yelled and screamed "these are first editions!" blah blah blah, to which I responded with "I don't give a F if they're printed on gold leaf, it's a joke you moron." She is probably now a member of the Supreme Court. That would be my luck.

Coming back from the dining hall and up the stairs, passing some jocks on the stairs and one of them calling me "whale tail". I made him sorry. No need for details.

Gwen and Denise winning "Best Couple of the Year" in the end of year dorm superlatives.

Me winning both the "Fossil Award" and "Best Personality". I think I might have paid people for the second one, I'm not sure.

Pizza Palace. LOL!

And then it was over, at least for some of us. I graduated that summer. Others with me, others behind me. But within a few years, we were all out of the nest, having left our mark on Scarborough and Towson.

And on each other. Susan was and remains one of the people closest to my heart. There is nothing I wouldn't do for her. I watch some of my friends' lives on Facebook .. where else. And I am happy to see that they are happy and successful. Some, of course, I've lost touch with. Some, like Tom, pop up every once in awhile to remind me not to take myself too seriously. And I love him for that. Gary writes a fantastic View from the Bus on FB that either leaves me scratching my head or laughing. Paul took the road I turned my back on and works for a television station in Baltimore. We share our miseries from the Communications department at Towson regularly.

Tom is the principal of a high school on the Eastern Shore. That one shocked me, said no one ever. He was born to teach. He taught me so much I can never thank him enough. Last I heard of Ed, he was a prison guard in Hagerstown. If you knew Ed, and his penchant for pistols, this was a good career choice for him. Mitch and Cindy married and split their time between their beloved boat and home. Wade is still the love bug he always was, and I may actually miss him more than anyone. Another one, like Susan, who faced very adult issues when we were in college, and more than succeeded, despite the difficulties. The Galligan brothers. I hope they're okay. Tim was a sweetheart, Jim was mean. But I loved him. Sorta. Just saying that 'cause I don't want to sleep with the fishes.

But my most favorite is he whom we know little about. Jim Froia. I'll end with … "hey, hey, hey! We're rolling now"

My Precious Son Turns 21

Today I celebrate the second miracle of my life … but it bears mentioning that April 27th is one of those just "happy across the board" days. Three of my favorite couples (Natalie and Ryan, Kevie and Julian, and Kim and Greg) got married on this date. And birthdays .. whooo boy …. two of the people closest to my heart, Kim McSorley and Alisa Kerns. I love all of these peeps with everything I am, and I wish for them nothing but continuing love and happiness each and every day of their lives.

But, today's post is reserved for the other half of my heart. Twenty one years ago today, my second child, my only son, Ian, was born. I'm not sure if I can ever do him justice, either on paper or in life. He is truly that kind of person.

Neither Ian's Dad, Rick, nor I knew if we would be able to have a child together. Before we were married, Rick was diagnosed with cancer, and underwent surgery and significant radiation. When I realized I was pregnant, despite great odds – believe me - we didn't know whether to celebrate or be very afraid that our child would glow in the dark! We decided to celebrate, and surely no other child was welcomed into this world with more love (except Betsy of course!).

I worked up until two weeks before my due date, and saw my doctor that day. She said she thought I would last the entire two weeks. I offered to pay her extra to extract this object. She declined. I was so done with being pregnant. I wasn't a good pregnant woman. And this kid, oh my god, how active WAS he? There was never a dull moment. And so the future was predicted!

The first week day I was home, I ushered Betsy off to school and Rick off to work, and I took to my bed to read a new novel I'd been saving. The windows were open, it was a glorious bright, sunny day (much like today) … and then … 26 or so pages into my novel. My water broke. SERIOUSLY? I am finally home alone and now THIS? Because Betsy had been delivered in a totally different way, this was a new experience for me, and quite frankly, not one I enjoyed. Best phone call ever, EVER:

Kim: Hello?

Kathi: Umm. I think my water just broke.

Kim: Honey, that's GREAT!

Kathi: Can Teddy come steamclean the carpets upstairs?

If you haven't been in that situation, that won't make you laugh. But if you have, you will realize that I was so stupid, I ran down the hall, into the master bedroom, avoiding two other closer bathrooms because they weren't mine.

So, I call the doctor's office – they are as shocked as I am since I had just been in 3 days prior and they wouldn't take extra money for delivering the baby then. I think they realized they had missed a sale. And of course they say "you need to go straight to the hospital, Dr. Dickman [Editor note: yes. On my kids' lives, that was the name of my OB/GYN] will meet you there".

So, I call Rick at the office. Now, you have to understand Rick. He is not really a giddy up and go kind of guy. He is methodical in everything he does. There is a plan. The plan must be followed. Sooooo .. I call, and he is in a meeting. I then call one of his co-workers and ask her to interrupt him. This, my friends, is out of the plan.

Sometime later he calls me back. Now. Those of you who have been through this ordeal (and I mean ORDEAL) can appreciate the fact that I was sitting there with a bath towel on my private parts. I want you to picture this beached whale and a bath towel. OMG. So awful.

Anyway, Rick calls me:

Kathi: Honey, my water broke. Dr. Dickman wants us to meet him at Holy Cross right away. The baby is coming.

Rick: What?

Kathi: [patiently repeats the above]

Rick: What? He's not due for two more weeks?

Kathi: Really? Tell him. And Teddy needs to come do the carpet upstairs.

See, the plan is FUBAR at this point.

TWO HOURS LATER Rick arrives home to take me to the hospital. The discussion that ensued between us shall remain between us. And several hours later, our beautiful baby boy was born. I'd like to note now, that while we are all basking in the wonder of his birth – the epidural only took on one side, so his birth was fairly schizoid – no pain on the right, chewing through the bars on the left. Motherhood is a joy.

Because Ian was such an active critter, he managed to wind the umbilical cord around his neck, and so was in NeoNatal ICU for a couple of days for jaundice and what not. But oh my goodness .. I honestly didn't know I was capable of such immediate love.

I worried a LOT that I wouldn't love Ian as much as Betsy. I as much as had that conversation with 7 year old Betsy. I told her then how much I loved her, that no one could love anything as much as I loved her. That I was worried I wouldn't love her brother as much as I loved her.

I was so very wrong. So wrong. I don't know that I can even describe the unspeakable love and joy I felt when I saw

197

Betsy holding Ian in ICU. I am sitting here crying as I write. It blows my mind and warms my soul that I have been so blessed.

Homecoming was wonderful, though bittersweet. Because of some breathing problems, Ian ended up on a SIDS monitor for six months. Rough time emotionally, but surely .. this kid was a beast in the strength department. Kicked out the bottom of his chair at like 8 months. Whoa. Plus, he was tall when he was born, and had outgrown the baby tub we got before he ever got in it. Then he pooped in his father's hand and peed in his own eye. Life … was VERY good, and I am so grateful to have shared that with Rick and Betsy, because they made it even more perfect than it was. Except for the brit milah, which WILL be discussed at another time. I promise you.

And so Ian entered our lives. And not one, not ONE day since his birth have I ever not felt over-abundant love and pride in my son. Among the things I am so grateful for is our ability to share with one another. Ian knows I am his mother, and he respects me as such. But he also knows that I try not to judge, and so we have been able to talk to each other over the years. Trust one another. My son has spoken in my defense, when I could not. I have done the same for him. He keeps me emotionally safe and afloat. I try to do the same for him to the extent that I can. He has another woman in his life, Michelle, whom I love dearly. And what the future holds for them .. I don't know, who can know anything. But I would wish for THEM that they would be able to hold a baby boy like I did. One who is compassionate, kind, sensitive, intelligent, and fun loving.

As a parent, it doesn't get any better than that. I am so blessed.

Happy 21st Birthday to my son Ian. I love you more than life.

And, son, everyone turns 21 and tests fate. Remember you have class tomorrow!

Bandaids

It's May. A third of the year has passed already. I wish I could say that this year has gone as I thought it would; but as is inevitable, it has not. Time is flying by.

I'm tired tonight, and I'm struggling with some feelings. Is it just me, or does everyone feel that when they make choices, they're just guessing what they're doing? I think it might just be me.

I spoke today with someone who has lived with an abusive spouse. It's the first time ever that I've spoken with someone who admitted to having done so. It was heart wrenching to me that my story was hers, because my story isn't a good one. Her story, blessedly, has a much happier outcome than mine so far, and I hope not to have to live it as long as she did. It's so hard to understand if you haven't been there, so it has been a balm to me to share this burden with someone who has been there.

Both of us fit the "part" of domestic (non-physical) abuse victim, and had it not been for specific circumstances for her (the abuser left the home and "freed" her), she herself doubts that she would be out of the situation. To hear her validation of the fear, the anxiety, the sadness, the depression of the abuse cycle – I'm not going to lie: Part of me wanted to scream "thank you" for the validation, I'm not crazy. The other part of me wanted to break down and cry forever.

There is desperation to being in this situation, a feeling of having to justify why you're here ("you're an intelligent woman, how can you not see what's happening to you"). But, of course, that's part of the cycle of abuse: you are made to feel that you cannot escape. And you can tell yourself that you are, but you're not really free. Until you're physically free. And even then, it's still in your head.

I know that as long as I am here, I am not free. I understand that. And I am still in the "victim" phase because I am allowing financial reasons to restrict my decision. I haven't let go as much as I should. But there's a reason for this. If I rely on that, I don't have to _really_ face myself. I tell myself and others that I am free of it, in my mind and heart. But if that were so, wouldn't I be able to walk away?

So that means a good talking to ... try to find the way off the hamster wheel. My heart hurts for my friends and family reading this. I know you would do anything to stop this pain, I know that. Some of you have told me that. And that's where the problem lies, and you know it, and I know it. I just can't accept it.

I'm not ready to free myself. I am still not worth it.

It's the damndest thing really. I'm working on it. Somehow, some way .. I will figure this out. In the meantime, I'll keep trying to like myself. At least enough to get out of this mess. I don't feel the least bit sorry for myself, so if you're reading this as a pity party, don't. I don't like myself enough to be a martyr! LOL!

This may be a bit raw for some people. But it's real. Believe me. It's real. And it's honest. If you don't want to read, please don't. Because this is a journey for me. And writing is healing.

Update: Miracles can happen. While this situation is far from resolved, I have reached the point where I am strong enough to face it. More importantly, my husband has faced it. It's not easy for him, or me. But my respect is beginning to grow as he, at 67, tries to discover who he is so that this will not happen again. I can't ask for more than that.

Do you ever feel like you head is going to explode because you're overthinking? I posed that question to my friend Scott, and I'm interested to see what his response is. For every molecule of emotion in my persona, his is logic and truth. So, when I feel like I'm drowning, I write to him and ask for his thoughts. He's never let me down yet (even when it was not something I wanted to hear).

But that's how I felt before I sat down to write. Like my head is a balloon. (veiled Pink Floyd reference there … name the song? Comfortably Numb. Great tie-in, except my issue is organic, not pharmaceutical and believe me, not by choice).

I feel so many things moving around in my head, I can't make sense of them anymore. How much do I say? Have I said too much? Does it matter what I say? Should I be paying a therapist instead of typing? On and on. And my kids, how much to tell them, how much validation do I need from them, or DO I need validation.

My mind is like a whirling dervish trying to sort through it all. I hate all this drama. I hate the nightmares that change brings. I hate the waking anxiety that promoting change brings. I hate the purgatory that no change brings. I hate the responsibility of having to make choices, even though I know that making them is a good thing for me though perhaps not for others. In short, I hate being an adult sometimes. No. I hate being THIS adult sometimes.

Why must things be so difficult? Why can't people manage their lives? I don't get it. I see train wrecks all around me. The answer seems so simple: love, respect, trust. Well, I have news for you, here's where the crazy train makes its stop: not a person I know would define "I love you" in the same way. Which makes relationships kind of a bitch. And I mean relationships of every kind.

My friend Terry said to me the other day that it is both a blessing and a curse to be able to think. I agree with that. But I need to qualify that as well. My husband "thinks", but his thought processes are not like mine. I don't understand them at all. Yet he agonizes daily, over thinking and trying to understand the wrong things. He is inert from thinking so hard. And he continues on his own personal hamster wheel from Hell.

So, over thinking can be a curse on many levels. Reason? Because over thinking is a result of "wrong" thinking (determining what it is you really need to be thinking about). Overthinking about the wrong issues incapacitates us. It prevents us from doing anything positive at all. If a situation is one that you should be addressing, options will come to you. But if a situation is one for which there is no answer, or for which the answer is harmful, your brain continues to overthink it trying to find an escape that simply isn't there. Overthinking should be a sign that whatever the issue is, you need to chuck it and start from scratch. Sometimes overthinking leads us into the land of knee jerk responses. These are generally not the best either and can land us deeper in the proverbial doo-doo in a heartbeat. So where in the thought continuum is the most efficient, effective place to be?

I don't know! I would be lying you and even worse, to myself, if I said I knew the answer. Because it's a personal answer. You can ask all the friends you want for advice, and feel like they're just throwing darts at the wall. No one can understand what is important to you. Except you. And until you are brave enough to discard the hamster wheel because you recognize that it will not power you out of the mental maze, you continue to overthink.

While most choose not to see it, it really is a "let go and let God" kind of thing. The stepping out on faith issue. It's so simple, yet so difficult. The truth is that we humans are always going to look out for ourselves, there is always a selfishness to our actions on some level, even among the most unselfish of us. Because .. good grief. If I don't look out for me, who is going to? That's how we process our days and nights. Because we feel like we have to. And so we add more reps to the hamster wheel with the addition of more things we need to take care of ourselves on. OMG. It's f'ing endless. We can stack and stack and stack responsibility on ourselves. And in doing so, we leave no room for us to live to our fullest and best. Why are we complicating things for ourselves so much? Because we are egotistical enough to believe that WE/I are controllers of our destiny. Ummm. Not for nothing, I'd like to say we are NOT doing good jobs.

I can't speak for you guys but I can't cure cancer, end poverty or tell you what our immigration policy should be. Heck, I still struggle with wanting to smoke. So I am not the all powerful Oz. None of us are the man behind the curtain. Yet we try.

I am told by someone I love dearly to stop blaming myself for the actions of others that I could not and cannot control. That alone, seriously, is an incredible statement. Let's break it down.

I am told: someone, somewhere cares enough about me to speak to me honestly. That's a plus.

By someone I love dearly: Do I even have more than five people in my life I'd say that about? Do you? So the fact that I have this person in my life, SCORE. Does this person owe me anything? No. I am grateful for their friendship.

To stop blaming myself: It's okay Kathi. You didn't do it. Think about this my friends. How HUGE is that … regardless of whether you can validate it or not, stop blaming yourself. That's emotional gold right there.

For the actions of others that I could not and cannot control: This seems a no-brainer. Yes? Still makes you want to kick someone in the nuts though, doesn't it?

My take: people will do things to you that hurt you, but you are not responsible for their actions or their words so stop overthinking how to make it better. How did Kristina's meme phrase it? "Chuck it in the fuck it bucket and forget it". Something like that.

My advice:

1.   Stop overthinking. It doesn't solve anything because if need to overthink something, you should chuck it in the fuck it bucket and find the real issue.

2.   At some point, stop the noise infiltrating your brain. More than anything, stop asking for help. Most of it is well-intentioned, but there comes a time when it all just becomes conflicting white noise.

3.   If you didn't make it happen, stop taking credit it for it. Good or bad.

4.   Ask for help from the one source that doesn't judge you. Take that advice and say thank you.

5.   Put those things that don't matter in the "fuck it bucket". Close the lid.

6.   Be happy that you've got the things you've got. There's a reason you have a lot, a little, or just enough.

7.   Buy a hamster. They enjoy the wheels. But you don't need to.

Mother's Day

Mother's Day is this Sunday. I am most blessed. Not only am I the mother of the two greatest children in the world (it's true and everyone knows it), but I also had the best mother in the world.

Not unlike most kids, I didn't always feel that way, and still today there is much that I'd like to change that went on between Mom and I. But in the end, my Mom was a gift that I never treasured as much as I could have.

My Mom died when I was 49 years old, and was, in fact, buried on my 50th birthday. I tell you this only as a frame of reference for this fact: I lived my entire life not knowing anything about my mother's life prior to her meeting my Dad. I believe they met when she was 26 or 27. "Not knowing anything" is not quite accurate – I know that she was one of seven children, was born in Sitka, Kentucky on March 17, 1923, and her full name was Daisy Kathleen Estepp. At one time I think I knew the names of her siblings, and I met one of them one time, and spoke to another one time on the phone. That. Is. It.

My parents met when they were both patients at the tuberculosis sanitarium in Sabillasville, Maryland in Frederick County. The very county I live in now. Apparently my father, who hailed from a comfortable home in Baltimore, was smitten immediately. His nickname for her was "Monkey". I don't even want to know. We found that out when we found batches of letters exchanged between them while in the sanitarium.

My mother's "life" began when she married my father. She always acknowledged the sanitarium experience, but declined to discuss it. The letters were buried away in the attic. Only incidental references to that part of their life were made. I don't even know where they got married. I only know that it was probably the best day of their lives.

My Dad hailed from a hearty German family. His own father died while Dad was in his teens. It was a blow for Dad, and he assumed the role of "father" to his younger siblings. My grandmother (who died before I was born) relied on him heavily. He graduated from high school, and then earned a degree in chemical engineering from Johns Hopkins.

My Mom was born in a "holler" in Kentucky. Her mother died when she was quite young, and there was a stepmother. She did not graduate from high school, and somehow ended up as a receptionist for Lever Brothers in Baltimore. This is all I know about that. Next up was her stay in the sanitarium.

After meeting my mother, my smitten father invited her "home" to meet his mother and sisters and brothers. I can't even begin to imagine how that went. My father's family, with a few exceptions, were not nice people. Snooty might cover it. And so my mother walked into the lion's den. She never spoke of that day. She did tell me that after her visit, she wrote my grandmother a thank you note. My grandmother received the note, corrected the spelling and grammar, and sent it back to my mother. If I show distaste for Dad's side of the family, perhaps you can begin to understand.

But Mom prevailed. She soldiered on. I don't know for sure, as it was never discussed, whether she told my Dad about those 20+ "lost" years. Even after her death, he remained silent on the subject. And that's okay. I respect their wishes. What pains me is that I was unable to help her. God knows that whatever the reason for her silence was, it had to be excruciatingly painful. I simply cannot imagine. And, if by chance, someone reading this knows the details of this, I do not want to be told. Please don't feel that you would be doing me any favors. You would not be.

I try to imagine how alone she must have felt. The Haacke family was ginormous. Because I was adopted, I too was rejected on various levels by that family. But, I had Mom and Dad to buffer me against the hate. Mom had no one but Dad. And he loved his family dearly – spent most of his life protecting and caring for them. That had to have been such a bitter pill for my mother. But she played the cards she was dealt with grace and humor.

I never felt close to my Mom. Believe me, I've been to therapy over this, I get it. I felt as though she might have seen me as a failure of hers on some level after my sisters were born. I think that might have been true, and what an awful place to be as a mother. I simply can't imagine feeling that way about a child, but I also do not feel anything but love for her. I believe with everything that I am that my Mom gave as much to me as she could. I think both of us probably would have liked to be closer, but it just wasn't to be.

I want to make one thing perfectly clear: While I may not have been close to Mom, there was never a doubt in my mind that she loved me. I think, if we could do it over, both of us would probably work things out a little differently, but who can't say that about some relationship in their life?

When Mom died, so many people spoke of her sense of humor. They still do. I had not a clue. Honestly. I wish I'd known that. My mother taught me to be a gracious hostess, to make people feel at home when they were in your nest. To be kind to everyone.

She also absented herself emotionally when I needed her but I know now that she did so to protect herself. She couldn't tap into something that would make her vulnerable. I get that. I never shared some of her values – I still don't. Some of what was important to her remains silly to me. But I respect that she held those values.

My mother set an impossibly high standard for me to meet with respect to love and marriage. This is one of those things I wish we had been able to talk about. She loved my Dad through her last breath, and welcomed him to heaven – I have no doubt of that. I wish she could have shared her secret for success.

My mother and I are not unalike. She buried her unhappiness and lack of self-esteem in substance abuse. I bury mine in emotional abuse. I never blamed her for her vices. Even though I didn't understand, something inside me told me to let her be, that this was how she coped. I just wish I could have helped her but you can't help someone who doesn't think they need it. And that may be one of my biggest life regrets. But, honestly, I never thought she needed me.

I know now that she did. Just as I need my children. I don't need them to do anything for me, I just need to know that they are happy and healthy and loved. I could have done things that might have made a difference. Or maybe not. I just know that I loved her very very much and I hope she knew.

The last thing I remember her saying to me, other than hospital words, was when I went to see her in the hospital as she began the decline that would take her away. I had colored my hair back to brown from blonde. She looked at me from the hospital bed and she said "there's my Kathi".

And I always will be her Kathi.

I love you Mom. Happy Mother's Day!

Bottoms Up!

So it snuck up on me, this stealthy awful gastro virus. No details necessary except to say that if I find out who gave this to me, I will hunt them down and breathe on them. If it wasn't enough that things at the office are being totally reconfigured, I now have this to contend with. Praying for a short stint.

Last Saturday night was Jason's farewell celebration. I must say that Alisa did a wonderful job with it. It was sophisticated and fun. I was afraid it would be an emotional two Xanax evening, but instead turned into a party till you puke event, with me tripping over an errant flip flop and falling down between the two beds in Alisa and Ammon's room. I did make it into the bed at 3:30. To say that it was a successful evening is putting it mildly. Sunday was recovery day (and Mother's Day – I am happy to report that I heard from Betsy, Aud, Ian, and Michelle, which made my hangover recovery period slightly easier).

Yesterday, back to work with old and new. One of the particular changes we made was the physical relocation of the original group I worked with into the building I'm in. So nice to see familiar faces when my two babies are now gone. It was a comfort to these old bones to have family around me again. Indeed, the work level is stepped up a bit because of Alisa and Jason's departures, but we will get through it and those in training will be asked to step up now and take the reins.

On Saturday night I had a very interesting conversation with my friend Matt. He and his wife Alyson are two more of my "kids", and Alyson is due with their first child, Hank, at the end of September. Alyson had gone to bed, and Matt and the bunch of us walked down to a bar to finish off the evening. Matt and I had a great conversation, as we usually do, but this time we talked a bit about my personal situation with my husband. Matt has a very large heart, and it was he who my husband insulted one night when we were out with them. I said at the time that it was like pulling wings off a butterfly. I would not have blamed Matt if he was leading the charge against hubby just on the basis of that one occasion.

But oddly, and compassionately, Matt made an interesting statement. He said "I just get the feeling that somewhere in Dave there is good".

I had to think about that. And I mean, I had to think about that. And, I had to agree with him. It's easy when you are a victim to overlook the kindnesses or attribute ulterior motives to them. I have always said that there was a tenderness to my husband that no one saw. Yet, in a disagreement, instead of waging war, he bludgeoned me with emotional jackhammers. It's hard to believe that person capable of love and devotion, believe me. I think many women in my position may feel this way. I would call it the cycle of abuse, but that is not what I am talking about. That cycle is defined: issue -> escalation -> eruption -> contrition.

No, this is something totally removed from the actual abuse cycle. I am talking about the moments in our life together where he has dropped the mask and shown genuine love and compassion. I was quite ill a couple of years ago and in the hospital in a great deal of pain. When he arrived, I put my hand through the bars of the bed and he moved over next to me and held my hand while we waited for the pain medication to kick in. Tears rolled down his cheeks for me. I cannot say that was not love or tenderness or compassion.

Our problem comes, I believe, with his inability to accept himself for who he truly is, if he even knows that person. I believe that over the years, he has assumed qualities about himself that he believed would project him as a more desirable person, when in fact, it did the opposite.

There is no doubt, none .. that my husband has been an emotional abuser. He wants to change that. But since my talk with Matt, I have come to understand that perhaps there are very valid reasons for it, and perhaps there are ways for him to learn to be himself.

He and I had a talk. I told him I was not the person I was a month ago, let alone a year ago. I told him that I did not trust him emotionally and it would take great time and effort for that trust to be rebuilt, if ever. I told him that I was willing to walk out the door today, if need be, but that I was also willing to see if he could come to terms with himself and me. There is literally nothing more that I can say to him that I haven't said over the past few weeks, or even that he could read here. He knows how I feel, he knows that I am not the monkey dancing to his tune any longer. He knows that I expect to be treated as an equal, and that I believe his bullying cowardly. He also knows that I love him, but that sometimes that is not enough. So, the ball is in his court.

Which brings me to me. Am I selling out? Am I giving into an old pattern? My own insecurities wiggled a little bit on that question.

My answer is emphatically "no". The reason? I am not a victim anymore. I would consider it a great accomplishment to be able to re-energize this relationship in a positive, non-threatening way. I go to my faith for help with that.

I also go to my faith to know that if I can't fix this very broken marriage, so be it. Regardless. I have "let it go". I am stronger and I am moving forward with my life, doing the things that make me happy, enjoying the friends I love so dearly – with or without Dave. It is his choice. I have made mine.

This is the right way to go – I have chosen well. Forgiveness is one thing. Victimization quite another. I understand the distinction and I will never go backwards. Onward and upward. Bucket list here I come!

Breathing Easier

You gotta be thinking .. she goes radio silent for almost half a month, and now two posts in one day? Yep. Taking time for self-reflection, allowing memories to come back and be enjoyed, and recognizing that you never stop learning has made me feel prolific. So, I am taking some time to share some of what I've learned over the past couple of months with you.

First, it has been a great learning experience for me, with help from most unexpected sources. Each and every one of you who took the time to listen and talk with me helped me more than you can know. And I mean <u>each</u> of you. You have given me food for thought, inspiration, courage.

Sometimes courage means staying a rough course, rather than abandoning ship. That is what I have chosen to do. But I am not the same Co-Captain I was in the past. Let me tell you what I have learned. I know that there are those of you in similiar situations who are struggling, I know that there are those of you who have survived similiar situations and prevailed. And I know that there are those of you who will stay in situations that could be better for you. Know that it may not be your time, but with every step, you get closer.

1. *No situation is ever perfect*. It's true. It may seem ideal on Tuesday, but by Thursday, the cracks begin to show. I

hate platitudes, and I'm going to use one negatively: the grass is _not_ always greener on the other side. Sometimes practical matters need to be considered, emotional issues need to be weighed. There may not be a "right" answer. There may only be an answer.

2.   _I am not responsible for anyone else's actions, thoughts, words_. At all. No one but mine. I don't know of a single person who doesn't want to believe this with their whole heart, but too often it is impossible for us to do. You are not alone. You are not the only person in this world who feels wronged - but the reality of the situation is that only you can wrong yourself. And you do that by accepting responsibility for that which you cannot control. And let me tell you - that's a mouthful of accepting right there. Why? Because of the impact of others on your life. Only you can choose how to process and run with information. Only you can decide that you won't be crippled by adversity. Only you can make peace with you. Remember that other's words and actions, though they may be hurtful, are theirs, not yours.

3.   _I am an incredible human being for accomplishing the things I have in my life_. No, I am not all that and a bag of chips. I will not win a Nobel Peace Prize, I will probably never be able to cook a full Thanksgiving dinner without help, I will never skydive. But the things that I do, every day, make me proud of myself. I can look in the mirror without looking away from my reflection now. Do you know how freeing that is? I accept now that I am imperfect, that not everyone will like me, that I won't like everyone else. I accept that my life is two-thirds behind me, and if it ended today, I could look at St. Peter and high five him. Yes, I've made mistakes. Yes, I've hurt people. But for the mistakes and

hurt that I've caused, I have given back in love and care. As have you, if you will allow yourself to believe it.

4.   *I am not bound by unreasonable self-imposed expectations*. Hard one here peeps. Who hasn't wanted to have the perfect life? Be the perfect size 4, not have their hair go gray and start wrinkling up like a rotten potato? Who hasn't wanted that financial security and the ability to do as they like, when they want to do it? I had to get real with myself. I had to take a hard look and see myself as I am - not as I wanted myself to be. I'm not gonna lie. I was a bit disappointed. I would be a hypocrite if I couldn't admit to myself that this isn't the life I really wanted, at least at this point. But I also take responsibility for my actions, both good and bad, that got me here, and I will tell you, that I did it MY way, for sure. I can live with that. I have learned many things on a spiritual level that I have no intention of imposing on you. But suffice to say that when one stops struggling against the tide, and hands the oars to a higher power, the feeling is impossible to describe.

5.   *I am proud of myself.* I am happy with myself, warts and all. But most of all, I respect myself. I have value - as each of you do. No more, no less. We are all precious and deserving of love. Don't ever give up on yourself, and when you think you cannot take another step, close your eyes and give yourself a mental hug. Love yourself and when you look back, don't see mistakes. Don't place or assume blame - accept.

6.   *I must continue on anti-depressants because, for reasons I do not understand, I still love the Dallas Cowboys*. Sad, isn't it?

I thank all of you who have given me your time and your caring to help me make decisions I needed to make. I feel that my life is opening up. I am going to stop being angry and upset and frustrated by the actions of other people. You guys are as big a mess as I am, I can't handle that AND the Cowboys. I say this with love.

But mostly I am going to love. I'm going to love me. My beautiful children. My wonderful friends. My sisters and daughters from other mothers. It's one step at a time .. a leap of faith. But the difference for me now is that I've "let it go". Truly. The past is in the past.

You get what ya need ….

Just got back from a weekend away with hubby. We went to Salisbury to play in a charity golf tournament. To be honest, I was so-so about the trip because it meant a couple of things: 1, I'd have to share space with someone with whom I was having difficulty liking, and 2, I would have to spend time with people who do not like me all that much. Needless, to say, while I embraced the idea of being away and playing golf .. well, the rest gave me a mild case of heartburn. Now, let me preface this by saying …. if any of the folks that were there read this, please do not make a blanket assumption that I am lumping you in with "everyone", but I don't think there is a single member of this particular fraternal organization in the State of Maryland that doesn't know that I have not exactly been welcomed with open arms, nor did I really try. So. Let's just agree on this. I give this background simply to frame the rest of the post.

We arrived in Salisbury Friday night. We opted to rent a car to go down. It's about 300 miles, and both of our cars have issues great enough that neither hubby nor I thought it would be a good idea to drive them. The cost to repair the cars that far away from home was greater than the rental cost. So, that worked out really well. I picked the car up, picked up hubby and we were off.

There is nothing fun about rush hour in the Washington/Baltimore metro area, so there's really nothing to say about it. There was a slight back up at the Bridge and again in Easton, but otherwise, smooth sailing. It was so nice not to worry about something going wrong with the car. We arrived in Salisbury, checked into our hotel, and went on the Club. There is just something about me and White Russians. They go well with a seafood feast, in case you were wondering. It's like mustard on a peanut butter sandwich. Some people can do it, some can't.

We met our besties Kim and Greg, and commenced the drinking and eating and general hilarity that generally ensues when the four of us are together. We go so far back, I don't think any of us remembers life without the other three. God knows there have been difficulties between us, and there were times when Kim and I would have taking turns throwing each other off a bridge, but when it all comes down to the bottom line, we'd all four do anything for the other. With that much varied history, the stories that resurface when we're together are the kind that can require underwear changes from laughing.

I didn't know most of the people in the Club that night, at least for the first hour or so. I do that when I drink. I'm a love bug. Or something. The reigning Empress of the Maryland FOE, Jackie, was there, and she graced our table with wit and charm. I can honestly say that this was the most relaxed I have ever seen her, at least with me, and I think I actually brought a smile to her face on a couple of occasions. This state of affairs is not the norm, and she and I have disagreed strongly in the past. Now that I am not a member of the organization, and no longer involved in any of the happenings, I feel fortunate that she and I have had a talk, and resolved (I hope) most of our issues. Jackie is a very warm person, and I am happy to be on this side of it. The other was not so great. Point one. *I never achieved what I wanted* to achieve in that organization, partially because I didn't have Jackie's support. So, I left it and went to another. And removing those barriers has allowed me to see Jackie as Jackie, and hopefully allowed us to see each other as friends, not enemies. Bottom line: what I

220

thought I wanted wasn't going to and *so I got what I needed*. A friendship.

To say that I dreaded being sequestered with hubby for the weekend is an understatement. To say that things have been tense, unpleasant, and all around shitty for years is also an understatement. But, in the past couple of months through writing and talking with others, I have come to a better understanding of myself, and my view of my commitment to my husband. I believed wholeheartedly that being "free" was what I wanted, and that's what I was going to have. Was our relationship crap? Oh yes. More than I can ever express. Was he emotionally abusive? Oh yes, more than I want to admit to anyone. I wanted to be free of him and his expectations. So, being locked in a car for eight hours roundtrip, plus sharing the smallest hotel room ever (there wasn't even a closet) did not portend well for my emotional health.

Shockingly, something else occurred. We talked. Ego aside. We talked. And I began to realize that the kernel of good heart I always believed existed in him, the reason why I had never been able to leave him, was not only there, but trying to emerge. WTF? This person who had never shown the slightest interest in anyone's wellbeing but his own was now talking. Not just talking, but talking from the heart. No bullshit. No facade. No anger. And admitting things. And telling me the truth for perhaps the first time ever. Recognizing the importance of things he never felt were important before. If you know him, that's huge.

For the first time in years, on Friday night, I felt like part of a couple. Maybe, truly, equally for the first time ever in our relationship. There is still a long way to go, and I am fine with that.

221

I am also in charge of myself, not him now, so whatever happens - happens. But I am optimistic for the first time in a long time.

So my second point is this: *I wanted to be free of my commitment to my husband*, I thought I had seen every facet of the same mean old buzzard. But apparently I was wrong. Apparently the heart I always wanted to believe was there, is. Apparently there is love beneath the surface of hate and resentment. Apparently there is something worth fighting for this relationship.

I did not get my want to be free of my husband, though I could have. Instead, I *got what I needed* - perhaps a chance to make the rest of our lives what I always knew we could do, but needed help that was withheld. It's baby steps. For sure. But it's a beginning.

Trudy you asked a question the other day. Do I forgive and forget? No, I absolutely do not forget. I have forgiven. But I am stronger and wiser now, with guidance from above, and I know that no matter what happens, I will be okay and happy. Were I to forget, I would make the same mistakes I made in the past. That's not an option for me anymore.

Peace.

Yeah. You've got a gang too.

I believe this may be one of my most controversial writings. Not because it's bad, but because what I'm going to write about is not concrete, not scientific, not a popularly held belief - at least that most will admit to. But bear with me. I think what I have to say might open some doors in your mind and heart. If not, that's okay too.

As most know, I have struggled mightily over the past few years trying to do the right thing, trying to make myself happy, trying to understand how to live my life. I did everything I could to change it. I'd move boulders out of the way if I could to get to something, only to find it was a wasted effort. I felt empty and shallow. My friends and family kept me somewhat buoyed, but there was nothing inside me. Nothing but pain and anger and rejection. And, of course, nothing was my fault.

I tried everything to find my anchor. I knew it was there, but it was just out of reach. My arm wasn't quite long, enough or so I thought. I would go to bed at night, planning out the next day. How to avoid bad situations, how to get through the day. Life had little meaning - I mean that in its fullest sense. It was just a series of occurrences and issues that I dealt with the best I could.

For some reason, my dear friend Liz and I were talking one day about mediums or psychics. Pick your poison on the title. We both have an interest in spiritualism, so I told her that I would look around and see what I could find. I've been to spiritualists before, boardwalk psychics are a dime a dozen. I'm not going to debate how the unethical feed on poor souls who really need their help. It happens. And it's heartbreaking. So, while I have

223

always believed there are those, perhaps even yourself, who can communicate with those on "the other side of the veil", I'd never really been touched by it. My head and my heart forbid me from believing this earthly presence is all there is for each of us. Call it my religious upbringing, call it intuition, call it crazy. But that's what I believe.

And so I set off in search (which means internet) for someone to speak with Liz and I. I'm pretty sure that I didn't get what I expected when I found someone. I had no clue what lay ahead. I had no way of knowing that my life would be changed in the most extraordinary ways, including writing a book. I had no clue that I would meet someone who would change my life to the point where I could forgive and forget, and move forward. And she did this with love and with honesty and the help of God [insert your word here] ... how could this ever be wrong?
Liz and I made an appointment to meet with Adele, who is a natural channeler, medium, psychic - everything. She describes herself as a visionary messenger. But, because I was still controlling my life, I sent a very snotty e-mail to her e-mail address saying that I thought that was a lot of money to ask for an hour, which I had no problem paying, but I wanted to make sure I wasn't going to get yanked around and told things that I could say to myself.

I got an e-mail back from Adele's assistant, Ashley, that said Adele welcomed folks like me the most, who were somewhat skeptical, but really looking for answers. I made the appointment for Liz and I. Something in Ashley's answer to me challenged me to think this might be the real deal.

Obviously I used Liz's and my real names. We had to pay in advance, you can't really do that with a fake name. Or I wasn't smart enough to. But I've googled myself a million times (haven't you? Admit it!) and there was basic information. Your life is not sketched out on the internet unless you share it, sort of like I am doing now.

We arrived at Adele's and she greeted us at the door. We were new clients, so she knew us only by name. Liz and I sat on the couch together, with Adele across from us in a wicker rocking chair. Understand that we were sitting in a condo, not in an office, not in a room "built" for table knocks, whatever. It was like visiting with a friend. She was outgoing, warm, and engaging, and any fears I had dissipated. I can't tell you why. I can only tell you that I was intrigued and a little excited.

Adele worked with Liz first, which I didn't really mind (though my impatience was off the charts). I'm not going to disclose what was said to Liz, that is her story to tell. But I did get a giggle when, after shifting in my seat, drumming my fingers on the couch, and bouncing my leg, Adele looked at me and said "Kathi, your energy has changed color fifteen times since you sat down. Relax. Your group is here and waiting to speak to you." She was laughing. My impatience is, by the way, notorious.

I will cite one example from Liz's reading, I don't think she will mind, but I want to properly frame this experience for you. When we left Liz's condo to go to Adele's, she said "damn, I meant to bring some water, I am really thirsty." I told her not to worry about it, that when we stopped for gas we could get her a bottle. Which, of course, it being Liz and I, we promptly forgot about. Halfway though Liz's reading, Adele stopped and said "I need to go and get you a glass of water Liz, your mother is really bugging me about it and she won't let me go on until I do." You draw your own conclusion. But I'm willing to bet this information was not available on the internet and Liz is the type of person that would die before asking a favor from anyone, let alone someone she doesn't know.

Finally it was my turn. We went through some really general things ("your mother said get your tissues ready", which annoyed me slightly because I am TOUGH and we all know that, right?) .. Then Adele looked me straight in the eyes and said "who is Diane". If you've followed along with me through this process of writing, you know who Diane is. But until that day, at that time, no one in my life knew who Diane was. It was something that only my family shared with me. A couple of other people, maybe? But on the whole. No. My hands flew up to my face in disbelief. Adele continued on to describe Diane as I remembered her, and then she told me how much I was loved. I have no explanation for this other than it's a fact. Period. There is no amount of research that anyone could have done to have known this to be true. In Adele language, that's called "validation". That she is telling you something that there is no way she could have known other than by lifting the veil. Mom was right. I did need tissues.

I'm not going to bore you with the minutiae of the remainder of the reading, but I will tell you this. In that one hour, my life began its major turnaround. I got answers for questions that I already knew the answers to but that could only come from my parents. I was so grateful, not just to Adele, but to Mom and Dad. There is no doubt in my mind that they were with me that day. They explained why I feel the way I do, and that I could change it. They reached back and shared information with me

226

that I needed to know to understand why they lived their lives as they did. And in some deep down place in me, I knew beyond a doubt, that I was saved. The things Adele shared with me weren't known to many, even Liz (whom I've known since diapers and we shared each other's homes growing up) was surprised by some of the things she heard. On some level, nothing surprised me. On every level, I was moved beyond belief. And motivated to turn my life around to benefit me. My loved ones and my "gang" told me they were always with me, and looking back, I can see that it is true.

For those who are skeptical, meh .. there isn't anything I can tell you that will change your mind. Especially if you have no belief in a Supreme Being, call it God or whatever you'd like. But I am here to tell you that each and every one of us has a spiritual "gang" who hang with us, keep us safe, allows things (good and bad) to happen when it's the right time, and that we do come around again. Your loved ones are not gone, they are with you all the time. You just have to believe. (Do I sound like Tinkerbell? If I do, think about that story. What happens when you believe? You can fly.)

Everything I have learned in the past year from Adele has been positive. I pray daily now. Never did that before. I thank those in physical absentia for their help and their love. I believe that the new track my life is taking comes from the bright little candle flame inside me, my own soul that I have finally taken the time to acknowledge.

My life is shades of pastel blue and white now. The blackness is seeping away. I am at peace, or more so, with the ups and downs of my life. Want to know why? Because I've given it over to those who know more than me. And by that I mean God and my "gang". I can't tell you what peace it brings to me knowing that I am safe. That I am loved. That life goes on after death, and mostly .. that I will see those I love so dearly and miss with every fiber of my being again. In a good place. Do you know how emancipating that understanding can be?

Adele moved me back to embrace the foundations of my life, the ones that my parents put into place 59.5 years ago for me. I was amazed at how freeing that was. It's so simple. Love one another as you would want to be loved. Really. That's all it is. Trust in something other than yourself. I guarantee that when you feel that burden released, it's almost a miracle.

I am not here to challenge your religious or spiritual beliefs. I'm here to tell you about what worked for me. Working with Adele over the past year has done more for me than any bottle of pills or high priced doctor. She, and my "gang", have challenged me to be my highest and best. I believe that. My work on myself has caused changes in me. I have severed ties with my sisters. It was the right thing to do, at least for now. I have the courage the stand up to my abuser and say "enough". I am working on removing the toxicity from my life. While I love all of my friends and family, and I thank you profusely for having my back all these years, I just couldn't hear you. I am so sorry, but please take this as my thank you for all that you've done for me. I hope that I can repay you in kind. But if not, you have my eternal gratitude.

Thank you my most wonderful friend, Adele. To say that you have changed my life, helped me open vistas that I never dared allow myself to see, and to feel my God with me is an understatement. You have given me the love, hope and vision I needed to live the rest of my time here to its' fullest. I love you dearly and thank you is not nearly adequate.

The Penultimate Chapter

Yep. I am wrapping this up for now. I actually have a deadline. I need to clean this mess up and make it presentable, though I have no earthly understanding of why. I've bled all over these pages, I've subjected myself to public scrutiny of some of the most intimate chapters of my life. More than that, I've set my ego out for anyone to dismantle.

Truth be told, I'm okay with all of that. If nobody reads this, then that is how it is supposed to be. It will mean something when the criticism begins, and I'm sure once I get past the hurt and anger and urge to cut everyone I meet, I'll find the positive. Actually, I'm sure of it. Nothing is coincidental.

Be happy peeps. Really that's all this is about. This thing we call life. There are miracles happening around and to you every day, you just have to be open to seeing them. I hope you do.

I wish you love.

Ha!

Gotcha all you ADD end-readers!

Acknowledgments

This is going to be the hardest part of all, because as sure as I'm sitting here, I am going to forget someone. If I do, please do tell me that I've broken your heart so I can strap you to the cross I'm already carrying, okay? Nah, I don't really mean that.

Yes I do. But know that it was not intentional. You know me. I have the attention span of a gnat.

First, there is a small list (I'm laughing about the word "small") of the people who have allowed me to be so honest about them in the book. You know, as does anyone reading this, who you are. I appreciate your trust in allowing me to share a story. I love you and I thank you for helping me make this happen.

Second, there is a core group of peeps who has cheered me on from the get go. If it weren't for you guys, I'm not sure I would have had the faith to get 57,000+ words down on paper. In no particular order: Liz Fleetwood, Ellen Baldwin Mielke, Krysten Gossard, Irene Saah, Donna Owens, Fran Monard, Kim and Greg Armistead, Susan Lundberg, Paul Jaffey, Pat Whitehill, Trudy Doleman, Terry Grant, Matt and Alyson Kline, and Dianne Morehead.

Third, to Scott Collier who pushed and pushed and pushed. Not by telling me what to do, but by being my friend 24/7 and throwing greater concept ideas at me, knowing I could handle it when I doubted I could.

Fourth, to Tom Callahan, Betsy Callahan and Joe Callahan for taking me into their home and their lives and teaching me what true compassion and wisdom is.

Fifth, to Alisa Kerns and Jason Smith for loving me even when it was difficult to refrain from smacking me upside my head.

And most importantly, to God and my "gang" for sticking with me, even when I pushed you away. Thank you.

Made in the USA
Lexington, KY
22 May 2014